IXL MATH WORKBOOK

GRADE 3
MULTIPLICATION
FACTS & FLUENCY

ISBN: 9781947569553
24 23 22 21 20   1 2 3 4 5

Printed in the USA

About this book

This book is designed for achieving fluency with multiplication facts through 10 × 10. Build your accuracy with the warm-up, and then increase your speed with more practice. Track your progress as you go!

WARM UP

PAGES 4–8 & 18–22

In these sections, you will multiply by one number at a time. When you are done, check your answers and write your score. Circle any problems you missed or that you found difficult. Review them.

Take as long as you need, but remember that things are about to get faster!

SPEED UP

Pages 9-17 & 23-52

Boost your speed! Time yourself with mixed multiplication facts up to 10 × 10. Write your time and score in the box. Remember to review any problems you missed.

Then keep going with the next page! Record your results in the Time & Score Log to see progress over time and set goals.

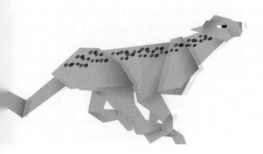

Bonus Features

 Take breaks throughout the book with mazes, puzzles, and other fun activities!

 At the end, get a sneak preview of multiplication facts for 11 and 12!

Time & Score Log

Page	Time	Score
Multiplying by 0-5		
9		
10		
11		
12		
13		
14		
15		
Multiplying by 6-10		
23		
24		
25		
26		
27		
28		
29		

Page	Time	Score
Multiplying by 0-10		
32		
33		
34		
35		
36		
37		
40		
41		
42		
43		
44		
45		
48		
49		
50		
51		
52		

Multiply.

$2 \times 4 =$ _____ $2 \times 3 =$ _____ $2 \times 8 =$ _____ $10 \times 2 =$ _____

$2 \times 9 =$ _____ $2 \times 7 =$ _____ $4 \times 2 =$ _____ $5 \times 2 =$ _____

$6 \times 2 =$ _____ $1 \times 2 =$ _____ $9 \times 2 =$ _____ $2 \times 4 =$ _____

$2 \times 1 =$ _____ $2 \times 10 =$ _____ $8 \times 2 =$ _____ $2 \times 7 =$ _____

$2 \times 2 =$ _____ $2 \times 6 =$ _____ $5 \times 2 =$ _____ $1 \times 2 =$ _____

$7 \times 2 =$ _____ $2 \times 9 =$ _____ $2 \times 2 =$ _____ $2 \times 8 =$ _____

$6 \times 2 =$ _____ $2 \times 2 =$ _____ $4 \times 2 =$ _____ $3 \times 2 =$ _____

$9 \times 2 =$ _____ $2 \times 3 =$ _____ $2 \times 5 =$ _____ $8 \times 2 =$ _____

$3 \times 2 =$ _____ $10 \times 2 =$ _____ $7 \times 2 =$ _____ $2 \times 6 =$ _____

IXL.com skill ID

94M

For more practice, visit IXL.com or the IXL mobile app and enter this code in the search bar.

Score

_____ out of 36

Multiply.

$3 \times 6 =$ _____ $3 \times 2 =$ _____ $3 \times 9 =$ _____ $4 \times 3 =$ _____

$3 \times 5 =$ _____ $1 \times 3 =$ _____ $4 \times 3 =$ _____ $3 \times 8 =$ _____

$3 \times 3 =$ _____ $3 \times 7 =$ _____ $10 \times 3 =$ _____ $9 \times 3 =$ _____

$3 \times 10 =$ _____ $5 \times 3 =$ _____ $7 \times 3 =$ _____ $3 \times 6 =$ _____

$3 \times 4 =$ _____ $3 \times 1 =$ _____ $3 \times 8 =$ _____ $2 \times 3 =$ _____

$8 \times 3 =$ _____ $3 \times 9 =$ _____ $3 \times 5 =$ _____ $3 \times 3 =$ _____

$3 \times 2 =$ _____ $3 \times 8 =$ _____ $7 \times 3 =$ _____ $3 \times 1 =$ _____

$9 \times 3 =$ _____ $3 \times 3 =$ _____ $6 \times 3 =$ _____ $5 \times 3 =$ _____

$3 \times 7 =$ _____ $10 \times 3 =$ _____ $3 \times 4 =$ _____ $3 \times 6 =$ _____

Score

_____ out of 36

Awesome job!

Multiply.

4 × 3 = _____   1 × 4 = _____   5 × 4 = _____   4 × 7 = _____

4 × 6 = _____   7 × 4 = _____   4 × 8 = _____   3 × 4 = _____

4 × 4 = _____   4 × 10 = _____   4 × 2 = _____   4 × 5 = _____

4 × 7 = _____   4 × 4 = _____   9 × 4 = _____   4 × 1 = _____

6 × 4 = _____   4 × 9 = _____   2 × 4 = _____   4 × 6 = _____

10 × 4 = _____   4 × 1 = _____   4 × 5 = _____   8 × 4 = _____

4 × 4 = _____   9 × 4 = _____   4 × 7 = _____   4 × 10 = _____

8 × 4 = _____   4 × 3 = _____   4 × 9 = _____   4 × 2 = _____

5 × 4 = _____   4 × 7 = _____   3 × 4 = _____   6 × 4 = _____

IXL.com
skill ID
5U6

Score

_____ out of 36

Multiply.

$5 \times 4 =$ _____ $1 \times 5 =$ _____ $8 \times 5 =$ _____ $5 \times 9 =$ _____

$5 \times 2 =$ _____ $5 \times 5 =$ _____ $5 \times 6 =$ _____ $4 \times 5 =$ _____

$9 \times 5 =$ _____ $5 \times 8 =$ _____ $5 \times 7 =$ _____ $5 \times 10 =$ _____

$2 \times 5 =$ _____ $5 \times 4 =$ _____ $5 \times 3 =$ _____ $5 \times 1 =$ _____

$8 \times 5 =$ _____ $10 \times 5 =$ _____ $5 \times 5 =$ _____ $3 \times 5 =$ _____

$5 \times 4 =$ _____ $6 \times 5 =$ _____ $3 \times 5 =$ _____ $7 \times 5 =$ _____

$5 \times 5 =$ _____ $2 \times 5 =$ _____ $9 \times 5 =$ _____ $5 \times 6 =$ _____

$5 \times 1 =$ _____ $5 \times 9 =$ _____ $6 \times 5 =$ _____ $5 \times 7 =$ _____

$10 \times 5 =$ _____ $7 \times 5 =$ _____ $5 \times 8 =$ _____ $3 \times 5 =$ _____

Score

_____ out of 36

Impressive!

DATE: ___/___/___

Multiply.

1 × 10 = _____   2 × 0 = _____   3 × 0 = _____   1 × 1 = _____

1 × 2 = _____   8 × 1 = _____   1 × 6 = _____   10 × 0 = _____

6 × 0 = _____   0 × 0 = _____   0 × 9 = _____   7 × 1 = _____

0 × 1 = _____   1 × 10 = _____   9 × 1 = _____   2 × 1 = _____

1 × 3 = _____   1 × 5 = _____   0 × 8 = _____   9 × 0 = _____

0 × 2 = _____   0 × 6 = _____   3 × 1 = _____   1 × 0 = _____

0 × 4 = _____   1 × 9 = _____   0 × 7 = _____   1 × 8 = _____

8 × 0 = _____   7 × 0 = _____   4 × 1 = _____   6 × 1 = _____

1 × 7 = _____   0 × 3 = _____   5 × 0 = _____   0 × 10 = _____

IXL.com
skill ID
CRE

Score

_____ *out of 36*

Brilliant!

Build up your speed! Track the time it takes to complete this page.

$7 \times 3 =$ _____ $2 \times 4 =$ _____ $1 \times 9 =$ _____ $5 \times 4 =$ _____

$0 \times 6 =$ _____ $8 \times 2 =$ _____ $4 \times 6 =$ _____ $1 \times 1 =$ _____

$6 \times 5 =$ _____ $2 \times 5 =$ _____ $3 \times 4 =$ _____ $4 \times 10 =$ _____

$2 \times 2 =$ _____ $8 \times 3 =$ _____ $7 \times 1 =$ _____ $9 \times 2 =$ _____

$7 \times 4 =$ _____ $1 \times 5 =$ _____ $2 \times 3 =$ _____ $4 \times 4 =$ _____

$5 \times 8 =$ _____ $9 \times 3 =$ _____ $2 \times 10 =$ _____ $6 \times 3 =$ _____

$3 \times 5 =$ _____ $1 \times 4 =$ _____ $8 \times 0 =$ _____ $8 \times 4 =$ _____

$5 \times 5 =$ _____ $5 \times 7 =$ _____ $9 \times 4 =$ _____ $10 \times 3 =$ _____

$9 \times 5 =$ _____ $2 \times 7 =$ _____ $5 \times 10 =$ _____ $6 \times 2 =$ _____

IXL.com
skill ID
DW5

Score

_____ out of 36

Time

_____ minutes _____ seconds

Multiply. Don't forget to track your time!

10 × 4 = _____   1 × 7 = _____   5 × 4 = _____   2 × 5 = _____

0 × 8 = _____   3 × 3 = _____   6 × 1 = _____   2 × 2 = _____

3 × 8 = _____   2 × 9 = _____   7 × 5 = _____   4 × 4 = _____

1 × 5 = _____   4 × 2 = _____   3 × 10 = _____   6 × 4 = _____

3 × 9 = _____   5 × 6 = _____   5 × 9 = _____   8 × 2 = _____

0 × 4 = _____   2 × 6 = _____   5 × 3 = _____   10 × 2 = _____

4 × 8 = _____   1 × 3 = _____   6 × 6 = _____   3 × 4 = _____

9 × 1 = _____   3 × 7 = _____   3 × 2 = _____   10 × 5 = _____

3 × 6 = _____   7 × 2 = _____   5 × 8 = _____   4 × 7 = _____

Score

_____ out of 36

Time

_____ minutes _____ seconds

Nice job!

Multiplying by 0–5

DATE: _____ / _____ / _____

Multiply.

2 × 9 = _____   1 × 3 = _____   7 × 4 = _____   5 × 1 = _____

4 × 8 = _____   2 × 6 = _____   4 × 3 = _____   5 × 9 = _____

0 × 5 = _____   3 × 6 = _____   5 × 2 = _____   8 × 1 = _____

2 × 3 = _____   3 × 5 = _____   2 × 8 = _____   4 × 4 = _____

1 × 10 = _____   5 × 4 = _____   1 × 2 = _____   3 × 7 = _____

2 × 10 = _____   1 × 6 = _____   3 × 3 = _____   5 × 5 = _____

4 × 6 = _____   2 × 4 = _____   0 × 10 = _____   1 × 1 = _____

7 × 2 = _____   8 × 3 = _____   5 × 6 = _____   9 × 3 = _____

2 × 2 = _____   3 × 10 = _____   4 × 1 = _____   8 × 5 = _____

IXL.com skill ID
87M

Score

_____ out of 36

Time

_____ minutes _____ seconds

Multiply.

$6 \times 3 =$ _____ $3 \times 1 =$ _____ $5 \times 4 =$ _____ $4 \times 6 =$ _____

$4 \times 0 =$ _____ $9 \times 4 =$ _____ $5 \times 10 =$ _____ $6 \times 6 =$ _____

$2 \times 3 =$ _____ $3 \times 8 =$ _____ $5 \times 1 =$ _____ $10 \times 2 =$ _____

$5 \times 8 =$ _____ $4 \times 3 =$ _____ $7 \times 2 =$ _____ $0 \times 10 =$ _____

$3 \times 9 =$ _____ $2 \times 6 =$ _____ $9 \times 5 =$ _____ $3 \times 3 =$ _____

$1 \times 4 =$ _____ $5 \times 7 =$ _____ $8 \times 4 =$ _____ $2 \times 9 =$ _____

$5 \times 5 =$ _____ $4 \times 2 =$ _____ $6 \times 1 =$ _____ $10 \times 4 =$ _____

$1 \times 9 =$ _____ $5 \times 6 =$ _____ $4 \times 7 =$ _____ $1 \times 10 =$ _____

$10 \times 3 =$ _____ $2 \times 0 =$ _____ $5 \times 3 =$ _____ $8 \times 2 =$ _____

IXL.com
skill ID
REN

Score

_____ *out of 36*

Time

_____ *minutes* _____ *seconds*

Multiply.

3 × 2 = _____   8 × 5 = _____   4 × 7 = _____   3 × 9 = _____

4 × 4 = _____   2 × 10 = _____   10 × 5 = _____   2 × 2 = _____

0 × 1 = _____   3 × 3 = _____   2 × 6 = _____   5 × 6 = _____

6 × 3 = _____   10 × 1 = _____   5 × 4 = _____   7 × 2 = _____

2 × 4 = _____   3 × 4 = _____   8 × 3 = _____   2 × 0 = _____

3 × 5 = _____   4 × 8 = _____   5 × 5 = _____   9 × 4 = _____

1 × 4 = _____   5 × 2 = _____   6 × 4 = _____   3 × 1 = _____

5 × 9 = _____   0 × 3 = _____   10 × 3 = _____   5 × 7 = _____

9 × 2 = _____   5 × 1 = _____   2 × 8 = _____   4 × 10 = _____

Score

_____ out of 36

Time

_____ minutes _____ seconds

Incredible!

DATE: _____ / _____ / _____

Multiply.

$3 \times 4 =$ _____ $4 \times 7 =$ _____ $0 \times 10 =$ _____ $3 \times 3 =$ _____

$4 \times 2 =$ _____ $8 \times 4 =$ _____ $9 \times 5 =$ _____ $3 \times 1 =$ _____

$7 \times 5 =$ _____ $0 \times 2 =$ _____ $4 \times 10 =$ _____ $4 \times 4 =$ _____

$1 \times 9 =$ _____ $5 \times 10 =$ _____ $2 \times 3 =$ _____ $5 \times 3 =$ _____

$9 \times 3 =$ _____ $6 \times 2 =$ _____ $5 \times 6 =$ _____ $7 \times 1 =$ _____

$10 \times 2 =$ _____ $1 \times 1 =$ _____ $3 \times 6 =$ _____ $5 \times 8 =$ _____

$4 \times 0 =$ _____ $3 \times 8 =$ _____ $6 \times 4 =$ _____ $2 \times 5 =$ _____

$2 \times 7 =$ _____ $1 \times 5 =$ _____ $7 \times 3 =$ _____ $9 \times 4 =$ _____

$3 \times 10 =$ _____ $8 \times 0 =$ _____ $5 \times 5 =$ _____ $8 \times 2 =$ _____

Score

_____ out of 36

Time

_____ minutes _____ seconds

Well done!

Multiply.

$8 \times 2 = $ _____ $0 \times 6 = $ _____ $3 \times 3 = $ _____ $4 \times 6 = $ _____

$2 \times 4 = $ _____ $7 \times 3 = $ _____ $5 \times 4 = $ _____ $1 \times 9 = $ _____

$2 \times 5 = $ _____ $6 \times 5 = $ _____ $4 \times 10 = $ _____ $3 \times 4 = $ _____

$1 \times 2 = $ _____ $7 \times 4 = $ _____ $4 \times 4 = $ _____ $9 \times 2 = $ _____

$8 \times 3 = $ _____ $2 \times 2 = $ _____ $2 \times 3 = $ _____ $7 \times 1 = $ _____

$2 \times 10 = $ _____ $9 \times 0 = $ _____ $6 \times 3 = $ _____ $3 \times 9 = $ _____

$1 \times 4 = $ _____ $8 \times 4 = $ _____ $6 \times 6 = $ _____ $3 \times 5 = $ _____

$9 \times 4 = $ _____ $10 \times 3 = $ _____ $0 \times 1 = $ _____ $5 \times 7 = $ _____

$2 \times 7 = $ _____ $9 \times 5 = $ _____ $6 \times 2 = $ _____ $5 \times 10 = $ _____

Score

_____ out of 36

Time

_____ minutes _____ seconds

DATE: / /

Follow the path! Step only on spaces with products less than or equal to 16.
No diagonal moves are allowed.

START ↓

3 × 7	2 × 5	2 × 2	5 × 4	8 × 2	7 × 1
10 × 2	9 × 0	5 × 6	1 × 10	2 × 6	5 × 7
5 × 5	2 × 8	4 × 10	3 × 8	5 × 10	4 × 9
4 × 7	3 × 3	9 × 2	7 × 2	4 × 4	2 × 6
9 × 3	4 × 2	2 × 3	3 × 5	8 × 4	3 × 4

FINISH ↓

Complete the puzzle.

Multiplying by 6

Multiply.

$6 \times 5 =$ _____ $6 \times 2 =$ _____ $6 \times 4 =$ _____ $7 \times 6 =$ _____

$4 \times 6 =$ _____ $8 \times 6 =$ _____ $9 \times 6 =$ _____ $1 \times 6 =$ _____

$6 \times 6 =$ _____ $3 \times 6 =$ _____ $6 \times 5 =$ _____ $9 \times 6 =$ _____

$2 \times 6 =$ _____ $5 \times 6 =$ _____ $1 \times 6 =$ _____ $6 \times 4 =$ _____

$10 \times 6 =$ _____ $6 \times 1 =$ _____ $6 \times 3 =$ _____ $6 \times 7 =$ _____

$6 \times 2 =$ _____ $6 \times 8 =$ _____ $6 \times 7 =$ _____ $6 \times 6 =$ _____

$6 \times 9 =$ _____ $3 \times 6 =$ _____ $6 \times 10 =$ _____ $4 \times 6 =$ _____

$6 \times 3 =$ _____ $6 \times 6 =$ _____ $6 \times 9 =$ _____ $6 \times 8 =$ _____

$7 \times 6 =$ _____ $10 \times 6 =$ _____ $8 \times 6 =$ _____ $5 \times 6 =$ _____

IXL.com skill ID

SX6

For more practice, visit IXL.com or the IXL mobile app and enter this code in the search bar.

Score

_____ *out of 36*

Multiply.

7 × 6 = _____   7 × 2 = _____   7 × 10 = _____   7 × 5 = _____

7 × 9 = _____   4 × 7 = _____   7 × 1 = _____   8 × 7 = _____

2 × 7 = _____   7 × 7 = _____   7 × 3 = _____   1 × 7 = _____

5 × 7 = _____   9 × 7 = _____   5 × 7 = _____   7 × 6 = _____

7 × 1 = _____   7 × 3 = _____   4 × 7 = _____   7 × 7 = _____

7 × 4 = _____   7 × 8 = _____   7 × 9 = _____   3 × 7 = _____

7 × 6 = _____   7 × 5 = _____   2 × 7 = _____   10 × 7 = _____

7 × 7 = _____   3 × 7 = _____   8 × 7 = _____   7 × 4 = _____

7 × 8 = _____   9 × 7 = _____   10 × 7 = _____   7 × 6 = _____

IXL.com
skill ID
9PT

Score

_____ out of 36

Way to go!

DATE: ___/___/___

Multiply.

8 × 5 = _____   7 × 8 = _____   8 × 10 = _____   8 × 4 = _____

8 × 2 = _____   1 × 8 = _____   9 × 8 = _____   6 × 8 = _____

8 × 7 = _____   8 × 3 = _____   8 × 4 = _____   8 × 9 = _____

5 × 8 = _____   2 × 8 = _____   8 × 8 = _____   3 × 8 = _____

8 × 1 = _____   8 × 6 = _____   7 × 8 = _____   8 × 10 = _____

4 × 8 = _____   3 × 8 = _____   8 × 5 = _____   8 × 8 = _____

10 × 8 = _____   8 × 6 = _____   8 × 2 = _____   5 × 8 = _____

9 × 8 = _____   8 × 1 = _____   8 × 8 = _____   8 × 7 = _____

8 × 3 = _____   8 × 9 = _____   6 × 8 = _____   4 × 8 = _____

IXL.com
skill ID
SMR

Score

_____ out of 36

Fantastic!

DATE: _____ / _____ / _____

Multiply.

9 × 3 = _____   5 × 9 = _____   8 × 9 = _____   9 × 2 = _____

6 × 9 = _____   1 × 9 = _____   10 × 9 = _____   8 × 9 = _____

9 × 4 = _____   9 × 3 = _____   9 × 7 = _____   9 × 5 = _____

10 × 9 = _____   9 × 6 = _____   4 × 9 = _____   9 × 9 = _____

9 × 1 = _____   9 × 7 = _____   9 × 9 = _____   2 × 9 = _____

4 × 9 = _____   9 × 8 = _____   6 × 9 = _____   7 × 9 = _____

9 × 3 = _____   9 × 10 = _____   2 × 9 = _____   5 × 9 = _____

9 × 9 = _____   9 × 1 = _____   9 × 4 = _____   9 × 6 = _____

9 × 5 = _____   7 × 9 = _____   3 × 9 = _____   9 × 8 = _____

IXL.com
skill ID
SUH

Score

_____ *out of 36*

DATE: _____ / _____ / _____

Multiply.

$10 \times 6 =$ _____ $9 \times 10 =$ _____ $5 \times 10 =$ _____ $10 \times 2 =$ _____

$1 \times 10 =$ _____ $5 \times 10 =$ _____ $10 \times 7 =$ _____ $4 \times 10 =$ _____

$10 \times 10 =$ _____ $10 \times 8 =$ _____ $1 \times 10 =$ _____ $3 \times 10 =$ _____

$10 \times 4 =$ _____ $2 \times 10 =$ _____ $7 \times 10 =$ _____ $8 \times 10 =$ _____

$6 \times 10 =$ _____ $10 \times 7 =$ _____ $10 \times 9 =$ _____ $10 \times 1 =$ _____

$10 \times 3 =$ _____ $10 \times 9 =$ _____ $7 \times 10 =$ _____ $4 \times 10 =$ _____

$10 \times 8 =$ _____ $10 \times 5 =$ _____ $3 \times 10 =$ _____ $6 \times 10 =$ _____

$9 \times 10 =$ _____ $10 \times 2 =$ _____ $10 \times 10 =$ _____ $10 \times 5 =$ _____

$10 \times 4 =$ _____ $10 \times 10 =$ _____ $10 \times 6 =$ _____ $8 \times 10 =$ _____

IXL.com
skill ID
6YD

Score

_____ out of 36

Awesome job!

Build up your speed! Track the time it takes to complete this page.

6 × 4 = _____   8 × 2 = _____   5 × 9 = _____   7 × 10 = _____

0 × 8 = _____   3 × 7 = _____   6 × 7 = _____   9 × 2 = _____

8 × 5 = _____   10 × 4 = _____   1 × 9 = _____   2 × 7 = _____

6 × 8 = _____   7 × 7 = _____   7 × 1 = _____   4 × 9 = _____

7 × 9 = _____   9 × 3 = _____   8 × 9 = _____   10 × 2 = _____

8 × 1 = _____   6 × 3 = _____   8 × 10 = _____   6 × 2 = _____

10 × 10 = _____   6 × 9 = _____   6 × 5 = _____   9 × 10 = _____

7 × 5 = _____   8 × 4 = _____   6 × 10 = _____   3 × 8 = _____

7 × 4 = _____   5 × 10 = _____   7 × 8 = _____   9 × 9 = _____

IXL.com skill ID
XT7

Score
_____ out of 36

Time
_____ minutes _____ seconds

DATE: ___ / ___ / ___

Multiply. Don't forget to track your time!

$8 \times 8 =$ _____ $9 \times 6 =$ _____ $7 \times 5 =$ _____ $6 \times 6 =$ _____

$6 \times 2 =$ _____ $4 \times 7 =$ _____ $1 \times 9 =$ _____ $2 \times 8 =$ _____

$8 \times 4 =$ _____ $10 \times 5 =$ _____ $9 \times 3 =$ _____ $7 \times 7 =$ _____

$10 \times 9 =$ _____ $0 \times 6 =$ _____ $9 \times 5 =$ _____ $3 \times 6 =$ _____

$7 \times 6 =$ _____ $10 \times 10 =$ _____ $6 \times 8 =$ _____ $9 \times 4 =$ _____

$8 \times 9 =$ _____ $6 \times 4 =$ _____ $9 \times 9 =$ _____ $2 \times 7 =$ _____

$9 \times 2 =$ _____ $7 \times 9 =$ _____ $8 \times 7 =$ _____ $8 \times 0 =$ _____

$7 \times 1 =$ _____ $8 \times 10 =$ _____ $7 \times 3 =$ _____ $6 \times 10 =$ _____

$10 \times 7 =$ _____ $5 \times 8 =$ _____ $5 \times 6 =$ _____ $3 \times 8 =$ _____

IXL.com
skill ID
EEY

Score

_____ out of 36

Time

_____ minutes _____ seconds

Multiply.

$10 \times 5 =$ _____ $6 \times 6 =$ _____ $7 \times 3 =$ _____ $9 \times 2 =$ _____

$8 \times 7 =$ _____ $0 \times 7 =$ _____ $8 \times 3 =$ _____ $2 \times 6 =$ _____

$6 \times 3 =$ _____ $2 \times 8 =$ _____ $9 \times 4 =$ _____ $5 \times 9 =$ _____

$9 \times 9 =$ _____ $8 \times 9 =$ _____ $1 \times 6 =$ _____ $2 \times 7 =$ _____

$4 \times 6 =$ _____ $8 \times 5 =$ _____ $4 \times 7 =$ _____ $6 \times 5 =$ _____

$7 \times 9 =$ _____ $10 \times 6 =$ _____ $9 \times 3 =$ _____ $10 \times 8 =$ _____

$8 \times 8 =$ _____ $7 \times 5 =$ _____ $6 \times 7 =$ _____ $9 \times 0 =$ _____

$10 \times 1 =$ _____ $10 \times 10 =$ _____ $4 \times 8 =$ _____ $7 \times 7 =$ _____

$9 \times 10 =$ _____ $6 \times 9 =$ _____ $10 \times 7 =$ _____ $8 \times 6 =$ _____

Score

_____ out of 36

Time

_____ minutes _____ seconds

Impressive!

DATE: ___/___/___

Multiply.

$5 \times 10 =$ _____ $6 \times 2 =$ _____ $10 \times 7 =$ _____ $2 \times 9 =$ _____

$9 \times 6 =$ _____ $8 \times 8 =$ _____ $8 \times 4 =$ _____ $1 \times 7 =$ _____

$8 \times 10 =$ _____ $4 \times 7 =$ _____ $7 \times 7 =$ _____ $6 \times 1 =$ _____

$2 \times 7 =$ _____ $6 \times 0 =$ _____ $3 \times 6 =$ _____ $5 \times 8 =$ _____

$4 \times 9 =$ _____ $7 \times 9 =$ _____ $6 \times 6 =$ _____ $7 \times 6 =$ _____

$9 \times 1 =$ _____ $9 \times 3 =$ _____ $7 \times 3 =$ _____ $3 \times 8 =$ _____

$10 \times 10 =$ _____ $6 \times 4 =$ _____ $8 \times 7 =$ _____ $10 \times 9 =$ _____

$9 \times 9 =$ _____ $8 \times 2 =$ _____ $9 \times 5 =$ _____ $5 \times 6 =$ _____

$6 \times 8 =$ _____ $7 \times 5 =$ _____ $9 \times 8 =$ _____ $0 \times 10 =$ _____

IXL.com skill ID TZ7

Score

_____ out of 36

Time

_____ minutes _____ seconds

Multiply.

9 × 10 = _____   6 × 7 = _____   9 × 5 = _____   7 × 2 = _____

2 × 6 = _____   9 × 9 = _____   0 × 8 = _____   4 × 8 = _____

7 × 7 = _____   10 × 6 = _____   2 × 9 = _____   6 × 6 = _____

9 × 8 = _____   3 × 7 = _____   6 × 3 = _____   9 × 7 = _____

4 × 6 = _____   10 × 5 = _____   2 × 8 = _____   1 × 10 = _____

7 × 4 = _____   9 × 3 = _____   6 × 9 = _____   5 × 7 = _____

8 × 3 = _____   7 × 0 = _____   8 × 8 = _____   10 × 10 = _____

9 × 1 = _____   8 × 5 = _____   4 × 9 = _____   6 × 5 = _____

7 × 8 = _____   10 × 2 = _____   8 × 6 = _____   4 × 10 = _____

Score   **Time**

_____ out of 36   _____ minutes _____ seconds   *Keep it going!*

DATE: _____ / _____ / _____

Multiply.

$6 \times 8 =$ _____ $2 \times 7 =$ _____ $10 \times 3 =$ _____ $5 \times 9 =$ _____

$8 \times 10 =$ _____ $9 \times 3 =$ _____ $6 \times 2 =$ _____ $3 \times 8 =$ _____

$5 \times 6 =$ _____ $8 \times 7 =$ _____ $9 \times 8 =$ _____ $0 \times 9 =$ _____

$8 \times 2 =$ _____ $6 \times 1 =$ _____ $2 \times 9 =$ _____ $10 \times 7 =$ _____

$7 \times 6 =$ _____ $4 \times 7 =$ _____ $7 \times 9 =$ _____ $6 \times 4 =$ _____

$10 \times 9 =$ _____ $8 \times 8 =$ _____ $9 \times 6 =$ _____ $7 \times 3 =$ _____

$6 \times 10 =$ _____ $3 \times 6 =$ _____ $7 \times 7 =$ _____ $5 \times 8 =$ _____

$10 \times 0 =$ _____ $8 \times 4 =$ _____ $4 \times 9 =$ _____ $6 \times 6 =$ _____

$7 \times 5 =$ _____ $9 \times 9 =$ _____ $1 \times 8 =$ _____ $5 \times 10 =$ _____

Score

_____ out of 36

Time

_____ minutes _____ seconds

Excellent!

Multiply.

8 × 5 = _____   9 × 7 = _____   6 × 3 = _____   7 × 2 = _____

6 × 7 = _____   0 × 6 = _____   5 × 9 = _____   8 × 8 = _____

10 × 8 = _____   8 × 3 = _____   10 × 6 = _____   6 × 5 = _____

10 × 10 = _____   3 × 9 = _____   7 × 8 = _____   9 × 2 = _____

3 × 7 = _____   7 × 10 = _____   1 × 6 = _____   2 × 8 = _____

8 × 9 = _____   7 × 4 = _____   4 × 10 = _____   9 × 0 = _____

4 × 8 = _____   6 × 2 = _____   9 × 4 = _____   8 × 6 = _____

7 × 1 = _____   9 × 9 = _____   5 × 7 = _____   9 × 10 = _____

6 × 6 = _____   10 × 2 = _____   6 × 9 = _____   7 × 7 = _____

Multiply. Draw a line between the matching answers.

6 × 4 = 24   8 × 5

2 × 6   4 × 3

2 × 8   3 × 8 = 24

6 × 6   10 × 3

6 × 3   9 × 4

4 × 10   4 × 4

5 × 6   2 × 9

Fill in the blanks. Multiply the two inner numbers to get the outer number.

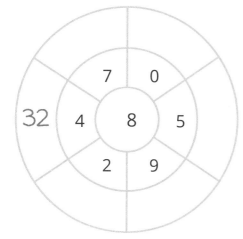

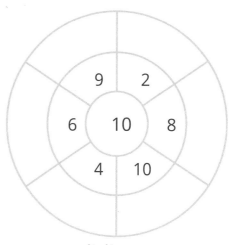

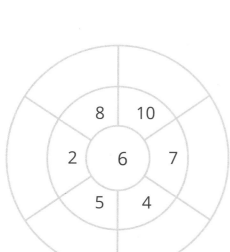

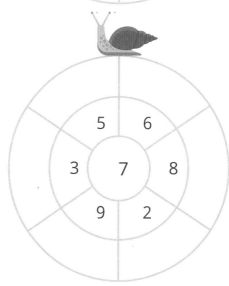

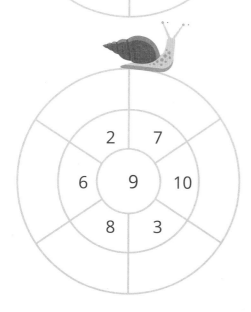

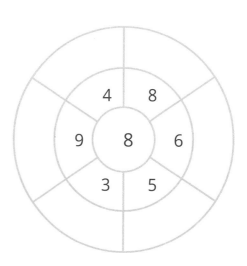

Put it all together! Multiply.

3 × 4 = _____   7 × 2 = _____   5 × 8 = _____   2 × 5 = _____

6 × 6 = _____   0 × 6 = _____   2 × 3 = _____   5 × 4 = _____

1 × 8 = _____   6 × 3 = _____   5 × 5 = _____   4 × 7 = _____

9 × 10 = _____   2 × 6 = _____   4 × 9 = _____   5 × 3 = _____

4 × 4 = _____   6 × 5 = _____   2 × 4 = _____   4 × 6 = _____

8 × 2 = _____   3 × 3 = _____   2 × 9 = _____   8 × 3 = _____

7 × 5 = _____   10 × 4 = _____   8 × 8 = _____   9 × 5 = _____

8 × 4 = _____   9 × 7 = _____   6 × 8 = _____   7 × 6 = _____

6 × 9 = _____   7 × 3 = _____   7 × 7 = _____   9 × 8 = _____

Score

_____ out of 36

Time

_____ minutes _____ seconds

Great!

Multiply.

$5 \times 3 =$ _____ $7 \times 6 =$ _____ $2 \times 5 =$ _____ $2 \times 0 =$ _____

$6 \times 6 =$ _____ $8 \times 5 =$ _____ $3 \times 3 =$ _____ $4 \times 6 =$ _____

$9 \times 6 =$ _____ $4 \times 8 =$ _____ $8 \times 6 =$ _____ $5 \times 9 =$ _____

$4 \times 4 =$ _____ $7 \times 5 =$ _____ $9 \times 9 =$ _____ $9 \times 7 =$ _____

$6 \times 3 =$ _____ $2 \times 8 =$ _____ $4 \times 10 =$ _____ $3 \times 9 =$ _____

$5 \times 1 =$ _____ $7 \times 8 =$ _____ $5 \times 6 =$ _____ $1 \times 4 =$ _____

$10 \times 5 =$ _____ $8 \times 3 =$ _____ $2 \times 9 =$ _____ $9 \times 4 =$ _____

$3 \times 7 =$ _____ $6 \times 2 =$ _____ $7 \times 4 =$ _____ $10 \times 8 =$ _____

$2 \times 10 =$ _____ $0 \times 7 =$ _____ $6 \times 10 =$ _____ $4 \times 5 =$ _____

IXL.com
skill ID
PNV

Score

_____ out of 36

Time

_____ minutes _____ seconds

Multiply.

4 × 2 = _____   5 × 5 = _____   3 × 4 = _____   7 × 7 = _____

2 × 7 = _____   2 × 3 = _____   10 × 9 = _____   0 × 2 = _____

6 × 5 = _____   6 × 7 = _____   4 × 7 = _____   8 × 8 = _____

3 × 5 = _____   1 × 9 = _____   5 × 4 = _____   3 × 8 = _____

7 × 9 = _____   10 × 3 = _____   6 × 6 = _____   8 × 4 = _____

5 × 10 = _____   2 × 6 = _____   6 × 4 = _____   3 × 6 = _____

9 × 6 = _____   4 × 9 = _____   5 × 7 = _____   10 × 10 = _____

8 × 5 = _____   8 × 1 = _____   7 × 10 = _____   4 × 0 = _____

7 × 3 = _____   10 × 6 = _____   8 × 6 = _____   8 × 9 = _____

Score

_____ out of 36

Time

_____ minutes _____ seconds

Multiply.

8 × 8 = _____   6 × 5 = _____   7 × 3 = _____   9 × 10 = _____

7 × 9 = _____   10 × 2 = _____   6 × 7 = _____   2 × 2 = _____

3 × 2 = _____   0 × 5 = _____   9 × 2 = _____   8 × 6 = _____

8 × 4 = _____   9 × 8 = _____   4 × 5 = _____   6 × 6 = _____

5 × 10 = _____   6 × 3 = _____   3 × 1 = _____   5 × 7 = _____

4 × 6 = _____   5 × 2 = _____   10 × 4 = _____   9 × 6 = _____

9 × 0 = _____   5 × 9 = _____   3 × 5 = _____   1 × 8 = _____

10 × 7 = _____   2 × 4 = _____   9 × 3 = _____   4 × 4 = _____

3 × 3 = _____   7 × 8 = _____   3 × 10 = _____   7 × 2 = _____

Score
_____ out of 36

Time
_____ minutes _____ seconds

Super!

DATE: ___/___/___

Multiply.

$3 \times 8 =$ _____ $2 \times 2 =$ _____ $5 \times 6 =$ _____ $7 \times 4 =$ _____

$9 \times 9 =$ _____ $6 \times 4 =$ _____ $0 \times 3 =$ _____ $8 \times 2 =$ _____

$8 \times 7 =$ _____ $5 \times 10 =$ _____ $2 \times 6 =$ _____ $6 \times 8 =$ _____

$2 \times 4 =$ _____ $8 \times 9 =$ _____ $7 \times 6 =$ _____ $9 \times 5 =$ _____

$6 \times 9 =$ _____ $3 \times 10 =$ _____ $3 \times 7 =$ _____ $3 \times 4 =$ _____

$1 \times 10 =$ _____ $7 \times 5 =$ _____ $9 \times 4 =$ _____ $2 \times 9 =$ _____

$3 \times 9 =$ _____ $6 \times 0 =$ _____ $3 \times 6 =$ _____ $10 \times 7 =$ _____

$5 \times 5 =$ _____ $8 \times 4 =$ _____ $2 \times 7 =$ _____ $5 \times 3 =$ _____

$9 \times 7 =$ _____ $7 \times 1 =$ _____ $10 \times 4 =$ _____ $5 \times 4 =$ _____

IXL.com
skill ID
3K8

Score

_____ out of 36

Time

_____ minutes _____ seconds

Multiply.

5 × 9 = _____　　8 × 3 = _____　　3 × 7 = _____　　6 × 6 = _____

7 × 1 = _____　　6 × 9 = _____　　6 × 2 = _____　　5 × 0 = _____

4 × 3 = _____　　7 × 9 = _____　　8 × 5 = _____　　10 × 3 = _____

8 × 8 = _____　　0 × 6 = _____　　5 × 4 = _____　　5 × 2 = _____

6 × 8 = _____　　4 × 9 = _____　　10 × 6 = _____　　4 × 6 = _____

3 × 3 = _____　　10 × 5 = _____　　9 × 8 = _____　　10 × 9 = _____

2 × 10 = _____　　6 × 5 = _____　　3 × 2 = _____　　9 × 2 = _____

1 × 3 = _____　　4 × 2 = _____　　3 × 9 = _____　　10 × 1 = _____

7 × 10 = _____　　7 × 5 = _____　　2 × 8 = _____　　4 × 7 = _____

Score　　　　　　　**Time**

_____ out of 36　　|　　_____ minutes _____ seconds　　*Well done!*

Complete the puzzle.

1 2 0

ACROSS

1. 4 × 5 = 20   **12.** 4 × 6
3. 5 × 10   **13.** 2 × 8
5. 10 × 4   **14.** 9 × 9
6. 2 × 7   **15.** 2 × 10
7. 6 × 6   **16.** 10 × 3
8. 3 × 4   **18.** 2 × 6
9. 8 × 6   **20.** 9 × 7
10. 10 × 6   **21.** 5 × 5
11. 7 × 5

DOWN

1. 3 × 9   **11.** 4 × 9
2. 2 × 5   **12.** 7 × 3
3. 6 × 9   **13.** 10 × 10
4. 4 × 4   **14.** 10 × 8
5. 7 × 6   **15.** 4 × 7
6. 2 × 9   **16.** 8 × 4
7. 6 × 5   **17.** 7 × 8
9. 5 × 9   **18.** 6 × 3
10. 8 × 8   **19.** 3 × 5

If you multiply across, you get the number on the right. If you multiply down, you get the number at the bottom. Use numbers from 1 to 10 to fill in the spaces.

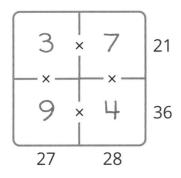

3 ×	7	21
× 9 ×	× 4	36
27	28	

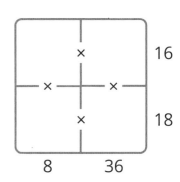

×		10
×	×	28
14	20	

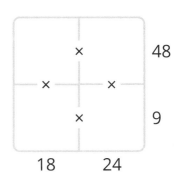

×		16
×	×	18
8	36	

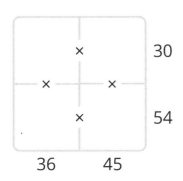

×		30
×	×	54
36	45	

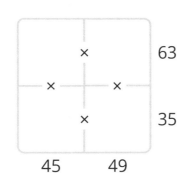

×		63
×	×	35
45	49	

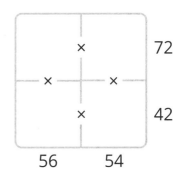

×		48
×	×	9
18	24	

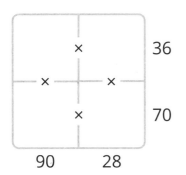

×		36
×	×	70
90	28	

×		18
×	×	32
12	48	

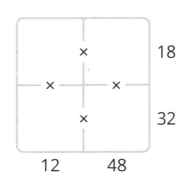

×		72
×	×	42
56	54	

DATE: ___/___/___

Multiply.

$4 \times 9 =$ _____ $6 \times 6 =$ _____ $7 \times 5 =$ _____ $2 \times 7 =$ _____

$6 \times 8 =$ _____ $1 \times 6 =$ _____ $9 \times 8 =$ _____ $3 \times 3 =$ _____

$9 \times 9 =$ _____ $3 \times 4 =$ _____ $7 \times 7 =$ _____ $2 \times 4 =$ _____

$2 \times 3 =$ _____ $5 \times 8 =$ _____ $7 \times 6 =$ _____ $9 \times 3 =$ _____

$5 \times 10 =$ _____ $9 \times 5 =$ _____ $9 \times 0 =$ _____ $8 \times 7 =$ _____

$5 \times 5 =$ _____ $8 \times 4 =$ _____ $10 \times 6 =$ _____ $5 \times 6 =$ _____

$9 \times 6 =$ _____ $3 \times 10 =$ _____ $4 \times 5 =$ _____ $10 \times 4 =$ _____

$0 \times 7 =$ _____ $8 \times 8 =$ _____ $7 \times 9 =$ _____ $8 \times 1 =$ _____

$2 \times 5 =$ _____ $6 \times 2 =$ _____ $8 \times 10 =$ _____ $10 \times 2 =$ _____

Score

_____ out of 36

Time

_____ minutes _____ seconds

Way to go!

Multiplying by 0–10

DATE: / /

Multiply.

8 × 9 = ______	2 × 7 = ______	10 × 10 = ______	8 × 4 = ______
2 × 6 = ______	5 × 9 = ______	3 × 10 = ______	6 × 5 = ______
7 × 7 = ______	4 × 4 = ______	8 × 2 = ______	5 × 0 = ______
9 × 10 = ______	1 × 2 = ______	3 × 6 = ______	6 × 7 = ______
3 × 5 = ______	7 × 3 = ______	2 × 3 = ______	8 × 8 = ______
0 × 3 = ______	4 × 6 = ______	5 × 5 = ______	10 × 7 = ______
7 × 5 = ______	9 × 9 = ______	7 × 9 = ______	5 × 4 = ______
6 × 6 = ______	3 × 4 = ______	4 × 7 = ______	10 × 4 = ______
3 × 8 = ______	5 × 10 = ______	2 × 4 = ______	9 × 6 = ______

IXL.com skill ID SUJ

Score ______ *out of 36*

Time ______ *minutes* ______ *seconds*

Multiply.

10 × 2 = _____   8 × 9 = _____   5 × 5 = _____   7 × 8 = _____

9 × 3 = _____   7 × 6 = _____   9 × 0 = _____   6 × 3 = _____

2 × 2 = _____   6 × 4 = _____   8 × 6 = _____   9 × 9 = _____

7 × 4 = _____   1 × 6 = _____   4 × 9 = _____   6 × 5 = _____

6 × 6 = _____   9 × 7 = _____   4 × 5 = _____   10 × 3 = _____

4 × 3 = _____   5 × 8 = _____   7 × 10 = _____   5 × 3 = _____

0 × 7 = _____   6 × 2 = _____   5 × 7 = _____   8 × 1 = _____

2 × 5 = _____   4 × 4 = _____   6 × 9 = _____   3 × 7 = _____

8 × 8 = _____   2 × 4 = _____   8 × 10 = _____   9 × 5 = _____

Score

_____ out of 36

Time

_____ minutes _____ seconds

Nice job!

Multiply.

9 × 8 = _____   8 × 7 = _____   4 × 6 = _____   8 × 8 = _____

0 × 3 = _____   3 × 4 = _____   5 × 9 = _____   5 × 10 = _____

4 × 7 = _____   10 × 10 = _____   2 × 8 = _____   4 × 1 = _____

3 × 9 = _____   8 × 3 = _____   6 × 6 = _____   6 × 8 = _____

5 × 6 = _____   1 × 2 = _____   3 × 5 = _____   7 × 9 = _____

10 × 9 = _____   3 × 6 = _____   7 × 5 = _____   3 × 2 = _____

6 × 7 = _____   8 × 5 = _____   5 × 0 = _____   7 × 3 = _____

9 × 4 = _____   7 × 7 = _____   4 × 8 = _____   6 × 2 = _____

4 × 2 = _____   9 × 6 = _____   2 × 5 = _____   5 × 5 = _____

Score

_____ *out of 36*

Time

_____ *minutes* _____ *seconds*

Multiply.

$9 \times 9 =$ _____ $6 \times 5 =$ _____ $7 \times 6 =$ _____ $4 \times 3 =$ _____

$3 \times 8 =$ _____ $6 \times 9 =$ _____ $1 \times 7 =$ _____ $5 \times 10 =$ _____

$4 \times 5 =$ _____ $4 \times 4 =$ _____ $8 \times 6 =$ _____ $5 \times 7 =$ _____

$0 \times 6 =$ _____ $10 \times 3 =$ _____ $9 \times 7 =$ _____ $4 \times 6 =$ _____

$8 \times 9 =$ _____ $6 \times 6 =$ _____ $2 \times 5 =$ _____ $8 \times 8 =$ _____

$2 \times 2 =$ _____ $7 \times 4 =$ _____ $5 \times 8 =$ _____ $9 \times 3 =$ _____

$10 \times 8 =$ _____ $9 \times 1 =$ _____ $2 \times 4 =$ _____ $3 \times 7 =$ _____

$7 \times 7 =$ _____ $6 \times 3 =$ _____ $9 \times 5 =$ _____ $8 \times 0 =$ _____

$4 \times 9 =$ _____ $8 \times 4 =$ _____ $3 \times 3 =$ _____ $2 \times 10 =$ _____

Score _____ *out of 36*   Time _____ *minutes* _____ *seconds*

Multiply.

2 × 2 = _____   8 × 7 = _____   9 × 4 = _____   4 × 10 = _____

5 × 9 = _____   2 × 8 = _____   1 × 3 = _____   7 × 7 = _____

10 × 10 = _____   5 × 6 = _____   6 × 8 = _____   9 × 6 = _____

0 × 2 = _____   4 × 4 = _____   3 × 5 = _____   6 × 7 = _____

3 × 6 = _____   7 × 5 = _____   9 × 8 = _____   6 × 4 = _____

8 × 1 = _____   10 × 9 = _____   3 × 4 = _____   5 × 4 = _____

7 × 9 = _____   3 × 2 = _____   6 × 6 = _____   4 × 0 = _____

4 × 8 = _____   5 × 1 = _____   9 × 2 = _____   8 × 5 = _____

5 × 5 = _____   4 × 7 = _____   8 × 3 = _____   9 × 9 = _____

Score

_____ *out of 36*

Time

_____ *minutes* _____ *seconds*

Super!

DATE: / /

Follow the path!

If you land on a product that is less than 30, go to the right one square.

If you land on a product that is between 30 and 50, go down one square.

If you land on a product that is more than 50, go to the left one square.

START ↓

3 × 6	5 × 3	2 × 3	4 × 8	9 × 6	4 × 7
6 × 5	6 × 2	5 × 8	8 × 7	1 × 9	9 × 3
5 × 9	7 × 6	8 × 9	5 × 3	2 × 2	1 × 7
4 × 6	5 × 2	7 × 3	3 × 4	6 × 6	4 × 4
2 × 8	4 × 5	4 × 9	8 × 8	7 × 9	5 × 5

FINISH ↓

Puzzle time

Fill in the blanks.

Box 1:

▰ × ⬠ = 15

▬ × ⬢ = 18

⬠ × ▬ = 30

▰ = _3_   ⬠ = _5_   ▬ = _6_

Box 2:

■ × ▲ = 45

▲ × ● = 10

● × ■ = 18

■ = ___   ▲ = ___   ● = ___

Box 3:

▱ × ◆ = 48

◆ × ● = 32

● × ▱ = 24

▱ = ___   ◆ = ___   ● = ___

Box 4:

● × ▲ = 20

▲ × ◆ = 70

◆ × ● = 14

▲ = ___   ● = ___   ◆ = ___

Box 5:

◣ × ▮ = 56

⬯ × ◺ = 28

▮ × ⬯ = 32

◣ = ___   ▮ = ___   ⬯ = ___

Box 6:

✚ × ⬠ = 54

▬ × ✚ = 27

⬠ × ▬ = 18

✚ = ___   ⬠ = ___   ▬ = ___

Multiply.

8 × 8 = _____   3 × 5 = _____   9 × 8 = _____   6 × 0 = _____

6 × 8 = _____   6 × 5 = _____   10 × 10 = _____   2 × 4 = _____

5 × 7 = _____   3 × 3 = _____   7 × 6 = _____   9 × 4 = _____

6 × 6 = _____   5 × 4 = _____   10 × 7 = _____   8 × 5 = _____

3 × 2 = _____   7 × 9 = _____   0 × 5 = _____   5 × 5 = _____

5 × 9 = _____   9 × 9 = _____   8 × 7 = _____   4 × 6 = _____

7 × 1 = _____   4 × 8 = _____   7 × 4 = _____   9 × 6 = _____

4 × 3 = _____   3 × 9 = _____   1 × 8 = _____   7 × 7 = _____

4 × 4 = _____   2 × 10 = _____   6 × 3 = _____   3 × 7 = _____

Score _____ *out of 36*   **Time** _____ *minutes* _____ *seconds*

Multiply.

$8 \times 9 =$ _____　$0 \times 8 =$ _____　$4 \times 7 =$ _____　$3 \times 3 =$ _____

$10 \times 3 =$ _____　$8 \times 6 =$ _____　$9 \times 9 =$ _____　$5 \times 3 =$ _____

$2 \times 2 =$ _____　$6 \times 7 =$ _____　$7 \times 8 =$ _____　$8 \times 10 =$ _____

$7 \times 5 =$ _____　$2 \times 3 =$ _____　$9 \times 7 =$ _____　$2 \times 7 =$ _____

$9 \times 1 =$ _____　$3 \times 4 =$ _____　$4 \times 4 =$ _____　$7 \times 0 =$ _____

$3 \times 6 =$ _____　$7 \times 7 =$ _____　$5 \times 6 =$ _____　$8 \times 4 =$ _____

$5 \times 5 =$ _____　$6 \times 2 =$ _____　$6 \times 9 =$ _____　$4 \times 5 =$ _____

$2 \times 8 =$ _____　$9 \times 5 =$ _____　$8 \times 8 =$ _____　$4 \times 9 =$ _____

$5 \times 8 =$ _____　$1 \times 10 =$ _____　$6 \times 4 =$ _____　$6 \times 6 =$ _____

Score

_____ *out of 36*

Time

_____ *minutes* _____ *seconds*

Nice!

Multiply.

$9 \times 9 =$ _____ $7 \times 4 =$ _____ $9 \times 2 =$ _____ $5 \times 1 =$ _____

$4 \times 6 =$ _____ $3 \times 3 =$ _____ $9 \times 8 =$ _____ $2 \times 8 =$ _____

$8 \times 5 =$ _____ $5 \times 9 =$ _____ $6 \times 5 =$ _____ $8 \times 8 =$ _____

$10 \times 10 =$ _____ $5 \times 7 =$ _____ $0 \times 4 =$ _____ $7 \times 6 =$ _____

$5 \times 4 =$ _____ $7 \times 7 =$ _____ $4 \times 3 =$ _____ $6 \times 8 =$ _____

$3 \times 0 =$ _____ $3 \times 2 =$ _____ $4 \times 4 =$ _____ $3 \times 7 =$ _____

$7 \times 9 =$ _____ $8 \times 7 =$ _____ $5 \times 10 =$ _____ $3 \times 5 =$ _____

$5 \times 5 =$ _____ $10 \times 4 =$ _____ $1 \times 6 =$ _____ $9 \times 6 =$ _____

$4 \times 8 =$ _____ $6 \times 6 =$ _____ $9 \times 4 =$ _____ $6 \times 3 =$ _____

Score

_____ out of 36

Time

_____ minutes _____ seconds

Excellent!

Multiply.

9 × 10 = _____   5 × 2 = _____   4 × 7 = _____   8 × 9 = _____

5 × 8 = _____   7 × 0 = _____   2 × 2 = _____   3 × 6 = _____

4 × 4 = _____   9 × 5 = _____   7 × 8 = _____   3 × 8 = _____

7 × 5 = _____   6 × 9 = _____   8 × 8 = _____   5 × 6 = _____

9 × 9 = _____   3 × 4 = _____   9 × 3 = _____   0 × 6 = _____

6 × 4 = _____   3 × 3 = _____   10 × 6 = _____   6 × 7 = _____

1 × 8 = _____   9 × 7 = _____   8 × 4 = _____   6 × 6 = _____

5 × 5 = _____   8 × 6 = _____   3 × 10 = _____   9 × 1 = _____

7 × 2 = _____   4 × 9 = _____   7 × 7 = _____   4 × 5 = _____

Score	Time
_____ *out of 36*	_____ *minutes* _____ *seconds*

Multiply.

9 × 6 = _____   4 × 8 = _____   6 × 5 = _____   4 × 4 = _____

3 × 7 = _____   10 × 10 = _____   8 × 5 = _____   5 × 10 = _____

5 × 5 = _____   5 × 4 = _____   0 × 3 = _____   9 × 8 = _____

2 × 4 = _____   6 × 6 = _____   7 × 4 = _____   6 × 2 = _____

4 × 0 = _____   3 × 2 = _____   8 × 2 = _____   9 × 9 = _____

7 × 9 = _____   6 × 8 = _____   3 × 3 = _____   5 × 7 = _____

8 × 8 = _____   4 × 3 = _____   5 × 9 = _____   1 × 5 = _____

7 × 6 = _____   6 × 1 = _____   4 × 6 = _____   10 × 6 = _____

9 × 4 = _____   8 × 7 = _____   5 × 3 = _____   3 × 9 = _____

Score

_____ out of 36

Time

_____ minutes _____ seconds

Fantastic!

Stretch yourself! Multiply.

11 × 3 = _____	11 × 5 = _____	6 × 11 = _____	8 × 11 = _____
11 × 1 = _____	10 × 11 = _____	11 × 9 = _____	11 × 3 = _____
4 × 11 = _____	11 × 7 = _____	11 × 4 = _____	11 × 9 = _____
11 × 11 = _____	2 × 11 = _____	11 × 6 = _____	1 × 11 = _____
6 × 11 = _____	11 × 10 = _____	11 × 11 = _____	7 × 11 = _____
11 × 8 = _____	11 × 4 = _____	3 × 11 = _____	11 × 2 = _____
11 × 0 = _____	9 × 11 = _____	11 × 7 = _____	5 × 11 = _____
11 × 11 = _____	11 × 10 = _____	11 × 8 = _____	2 × 11 = _____
9 × 11 = _____	1 × 11 = _____	11 × 5 = _____	6 × 11 = _____

Multiplying by 12

DATE: _____ / _____ / _____

Multiply.

1 × 12 = _____	12 × 4 = _____	12 × 2 = _____	6 × 12 = _____
7 × 12 = _____	8 × 12 = _____	1 × 12 = _____	10 × 12 = _____
2 × 12 = _____	12 × 7 = _____	3 × 12 = _____	0 × 12 = _____
6 × 12 = _____	12 × 1 = _____	12 × 9 = _____	12 × 8 = _____
4 × 12 = _____	11 × 12 = _____	12 × 3 = _____	12 × 5 = _____
12 × 9 = _____	12 × 12 = _____	5 × 12 = _____	12 × 3 = _____
12 × 12 = _____	12 × 8 = _____	4 × 12 = _____	0 × 12 = _____
9 × 12 = _____	12 × 10 = _____	12 × 5 = _____	12 × 6 = _____
3 × 12 = _____	12 × 0 = _____	12 × 11 = _____	2 × 12 = _____

IXL.com
skill ID
8NV

Score

_____ *out of 36*

Incredible!

Multiply.

12 × 6 = _____   6 × 11 = _____   9 × 12 = _____   12 × 0 = _____

7 × 11 = _____   12 × 11 = _____   0 × 12 = _____   9 × 11 = _____

11 × 5 = _____   11 × 2 = _____   12 × 7 = _____   0 × 11 = _____

1 × 12 = _____   11 × 11 = _____   2 × 11 = _____   5 × 12 = _____

12 × 12 = _____   11 × 7 = _____   11 × 12 = _____   4 × 11 = _____

11 × 1 = _____   12 × 3 = _____   12 × 8 = _____   12 × 10 = _____

11 × 11 = _____   12 × 2 = _____   6 × 12 = _____   8 × 12 = _____

12 × 4 = _____   11 × 4 = _____   3 × 12 = _____   11 × 9 = _____

8 × 11 = _____   7 × 12 = _____   10 × 11 = _____   12 × 12 = _____

IXL.com
skill ID
TK7

Score

_____ out of 36

Multiply.

12 × 8 = _____   0 × 12 = _____   12 × 12 = _____   7 × 11 = _____

1 × 11 = _____   12 × 6 = _____   11 × 10 = _____   12 × 9 = _____

11 × 7 = _____   12 × 7 = _____   11 × 11 = _____   11 × 4 = _____

12 × 1 = _____   11 × 0 = _____   12 × 5 = _____   12 × 12 = _____

11 × 8 = _____   6 × 12 = _____   12 × 0 = _____   11 × 6 = _____

10 × 12 = _____   12 × 4 = _____   11 × 1 = _____   2 × 12 = _____

3 × 11 = _____   11 × 12 = _____   9 × 11 = _____   11 × 5 = _____

12 × 2 = _____   11 × 9 = _____   4 × 12 = _____   11 × 2 = _____

12 × 3 = _____   5 × 11 = _____   12 × 11 = _____   8 × 12 = _____

IXL.com
skill ID
YSY

Score

_____ out of 36

Great!

Answer key

PAGE 4

$2 \times 4 = 8$	$2 \times 3 = 6$	$2 \times 8 = 16$	$10 \times 2 = 20$
$2 \times 9 = 18$	$2 \times 7 = 14$	$4 \times 2 = 8$	$5 \times 2 = 10$
$6 \times 2 = 12$	$1 \times 2 = 2$	$9 \times 2 = 18$	$2 \times 4 = 8$
$2 \times 1 = 2$	$2 \times 10 = 20$	$8 \times 2 = 16$	$2 \times 7 = 14$
$2 \times 2 = 4$	$2 \times 6 = 12$	$5 \times 2 = 10$	$1 \times 2 = 2$
$7 \times 2 = 14$	$2 \times 9 = 18$	$2 \times 2 = 4$	$2 \times 8 = 16$
$6 \times 2 = 12$	$2 \times 2 = 4$	$4 \times 2 = 8$	$3 \times 2 = 6$
$9 \times 2 = 18$	$2 \times 3 = 6$	$2 \times 5 = 10$	$8 \times 2 = 16$
$3 \times 2 = 6$	$10 \times 2 = 20$	$7 \times 2 = 14$	$2 \times 6 = 12$

PAGE 5

$3 \times 6 = 18$	$3 \times 2 = 6$	$3 \times 9 = 27$	$4 \times 3 = 12$
$3 \times 5 = 15$	$1 \times 3 = 3$	$4 \times 3 = 12$	$3 \times 8 = 24$
$3 \times 3 = 9$	$3 \times 7 = 21$	$10 \times 3 = 30$	$9 \times 3 = 27$
$3 \times 10 = 30$	$5 \times 3 = 15$	$7 \times 3 = 21$	$3 \times 6 = 18$
$3 \times 4 = 12$	$3 \times 1 = 3$	$3 \times 8 = 24$	$2 \times 3 = 6$
$8 \times 3 = 24$	$3 \times 9 = 27$	$3 \times 5 = 15$	$3 \times 3 = 9$
$3 \times 2 = 6$	$3 \times 8 = 24$	$7 \times 3 = 21$	$3 \times 1 = 3$
$9 \times 3 = 27$	$3 \times 3 = 9$	$6 \times 3 = 18$	$5 \times 3 = 15$
$3 \times 7 = 21$	$10 \times 3 = 30$	$3 \times 4 = 12$	$3 \times 6 = 18$

PAGE 6

$4 \times 3 = 12$	$1 \times 4 = 4$	$5 \times 4 = 20$	$4 \times 7 = 28$
$4 \times 6 = 24$	$7 \times 4 = 28$	$4 \times 8 = 32$	$3 \times 4 = 12$
$4 \times 4 = 16$	$4 \times 10 = 40$	$4 \times 2 = 8$	$4 \times 5 = 20$
$4 \times 7 = 28$	$4 \times 4 = 16$	$9 \times 4 = 36$	$4 \times 1 = 4$
$6 \times 4 = 24$	$4 \times 9 = 36$	$2 \times 4 = 8$	$4 \times 6 = 24$
$10 \times 4 = 40$	$4 \times 1 = 4$	$4 \times 5 = 20$	$8 \times 4 = 32$
$4 \times 4 = 16$	$9 \times 4 = 36$	$4 \times 7 = 28$	$4 \times 10 = 40$
$8 \times 4 = 32$	$4 \times 3 = 12$	$4 \times 9 = 36$	$4 \times 2 = 8$
$5 \times 4 = 20$	$4 \times 7 = 28$	$3 \times 4 = 12$	$6 \times 4 = 24$

PAGE 7

$5 \times 4 = 20$	$1 \times 5 = 5$	$8 \times 5 = 40$	$5 \times 9 = 45$
$5 \times 2 = 10$	$5 \times 5 = 25$	$5 \times 6 = 30$	$4 \times 5 = 20$
$9 \times 5 = 45$	$5 \times 8 = 40$	$5 \times 7 = 35$	$5 \times 10 = 50$
$2 \times 5 = 10$	$5 \times 4 = 20$	$5 \times 3 = 15$	$5 \times 1 = 5$
$8 \times 5 = 40$	$10 \times 5 = 50$	$5 \times 5 = 25$	$3 \times 5 = 15$
$5 \times 4 = 20$	$6 \times 5 = 30$	$3 \times 5 = 15$	$7 \times 5 = 35$
$5 \times 5 = 25$	$2 \times 5 = 10$	$9 \times 5 = 45$	$5 \times 6 = 30$
$5 \times 1 = 5$	$5 \times 9 = 45$	$6 \times 5 = 30$	$5 \times 7 = 35$
$10 \times 5 = 50$	$7 \times 5 = 35$	$5 \times 8 = 40$	$3 \times 5 = 15$

PAGE 8

$1 \times 10 = 10$	$2 \times 0 = 0$	$3 \times 0 = 0$	$1 \times 1 = 1$
$1 \times 2 = 2$	$8 \times 1 = 8$	$1 \times 6 = 6$	$10 \times 0 = 0$
$6 \times 0 = 0$	$0 \times 0 = 0$	$0 \times 9 = 0$	$7 \times 1 = 7$
$0 \times 1 = 0$	$1 \times 10 = 10$	$9 \times 1 = 9$	$2 \times 1 = 2$
$1 \times 3 = 3$	$1 \times 5 = 5$	$0 \times 8 = 0$	$9 \times 0 = 0$
$0 \times 2 = 0$	$0 \times 6 = 0$	$3 \times 1 = 3$	$1 \times 0 = 0$
$0 \times 4 = 0$	$1 \times 9 = 9$	$0 \times 7 = 0$	$1 \times 8 = 8$
$8 \times 0 = 0$	$7 \times 0 = 0$	$4 \times 1 = 4$	$6 \times 1 = 6$
$1 \times 7 = 7$	$0 \times 3 = 0$	$5 \times 0 = 0$	$0 \times 10 = 0$

PAGE 9

$7 \times 3 = 21$	$2 \times 4 = 8$	$1 \times 9 = 9$	$5 \times 4 = 20$
$0 \times 6 = 0$	$8 \times 2 = 16$	$4 \times 6 = 24$	$1 \times 1 = 1$
$6 \times 5 = 30$	$2 \times 5 = 10$	$3 \times 4 = 12$	$4 \times 10 = 40$
$2 \times 2 = 4$	$8 \times 3 = 24$	$7 \times 1 = 7$	$9 \times 2 = 18$
$7 \times 4 = 28$	$1 \times 5 = 5$	$2 \times 3 = 6$	$4 \times 4 = 16$
$5 \times 8 = 40$	$9 \times 3 = 27$	$2 \times 10 = 20$	$6 \times 3 = 18$
$3 \times 5 = 15$	$1 \times 4 = 4$	$8 \times 0 = 0$	$8 \times 4 = 32$
$5 \times 5 = 25$	$5 \times 7 = 35$	$9 \times 4 = 36$	$10 \times 3 = 30$
$9 \times 5 = 45$	$2 \times 7 = 14$	$5 \times 10 = 50$	$6 \times 2 = 12$

PAGE 10

$10 \times 4 = 40$	$1 \times 7 = 7$	$5 \times 4 = 20$	$2 \times 5 = 10$
$0 \times 8 = 0$	$3 \times 3 = 9$	$6 \times 1 = 6$	$2 \times 2 = 4$
$3 \times 8 = 24$	$2 \times 9 = 18$	$7 \times 5 = 35$	$4 \times 4 = 16$
$1 \times 5 = 5$	$4 \times 2 = 8$	$3 \times 10 = 30$	$6 \times 4 = 24$
$3 \times 9 = 27$	$5 \times 6 = 30$	$5 \times 9 = 45$	$8 \times 2 = 16$
$0 \times 4 = 0$	$2 \times 6 = 12$	$5 \times 3 = 15$	$10 \times 2 = 20$
$4 \times 8 = 32$	$1 \times 3 = 3$	$6 \times 6 = 36$	$3 \times 4 = 12$
$9 \times 1 = 9$	$3 \times 7 = 21$	$3 \times 2 = 6$	$10 \times 5 = 50$
$3 \times 6 = 18$	$7 \times 2 = 14$	$5 \times 8 = 40$	$4 \times 7 = 28$

PAGE 11

$2 \times 9 = 18$	$1 \times 3 = 3$	$7 \times 4 = 28$	$5 \times 1 = 5$
$4 \times 8 = 32$	$2 \times 6 = 12$	$4 \times 3 = 12$	$5 \times 9 = 45$
$0 \times 5 = 0$	$3 \times 6 = 18$	$5 \times 2 = 10$	$8 \times 1 = 8$
$2 \times 3 = 6$	$3 \times 5 = 15$	$2 \times 8 = 16$	$4 \times 4 = 16$
$1 \times 10 = 10$	$5 \times 4 = 20$	$1 \times 2 = 2$	$3 \times 7 = 21$
$2 \times 10 = 20$	$1 \times 6 = 6$	$3 \times 3 = 9$	$5 \times 5 = 25$
$4 \times 6 = 24$	$2 \times 4 = 8$	$0 \times 10 = 0$	$1 \times 1 = 1$
$7 \times 2 = 14$	$8 \times 3 = 24$	$5 \times 6 = 30$	$9 \times 3 = 27$
$2 \times 2 = 4$	$3 \times 10 = 30$	$4 \times 1 = 4$	$8 \times 5 = 40$

Answer key

PAGE 12

6 × 3 = 18	3 × 1 = 3	5 × 4 = 20	4 × 6 = 24
4 × 0 = 0	9 × 4 = 36	5 × 10 = 50	6 × 6 = 36
2 × 3 = 6	3 × 8 = 24	5 × 1 = 5	10 × 2 = 20
5 × 8 = 40	4 × 3 = 12	7 × 2 = 14	0 × 10 = 0
3 × 9 = 27	2 × 6 = 12	9 × 5 = 45	3 × 3 = 9
1 × 4 = 4	5 × 7 = 35	8 × 4 = 32	2 × 9 = 18
5 × 5 = 25	4 × 2 = 8	6 × 1 = 6	10 × 4 = 40
1 × 9 = 9	5 × 6 = 30	4 × 7 = 28	1 × 10 = 10
10 × 3 = 30	2 × 0 = 0	5 × 3 = 15	8 × 2 = 16

PAGE 13

3 × 2 = 6	8 × 5 = 40	4 × 7 = 28	3 × 9 = 27
4 × 4 = 16	2 × 10 = 20	10 × 5 = 50	2 × 2 = 4
0 × 1 = 0	3 × 3 = 9	2 × 6 = 12	5 × 6 = 30
6 × 3 = 18	10 × 1 = 10	5 × 4 = 20	7 × 2 = 14
2 × 4 = 8	3 × 4 = 12	8 × 3 = 24	2 × 0 = 0
3 × 5 = 15	4 × 8 = 32	5 × 5 = 25	9 × 4 = 36
1 × 4 = 4	5 × 2 = 10	6 × 4 = 24	3 × 1 = 3
5 × 9 = 45	0 × 3 = 0	10 × 3 = 30	5 × 7 = 35
9 × 2 = 18	5 × 1 = 5	2 × 8 = 16	4 × 10 = 40

PAGE 14

3 × 4 = 12	4 × 7 = 28	0 × 10 = 0	3 × 3 = 9
4 × 2 = 8	8 × 4 = 32	9 × 5 = 45	3 × 1 = 3
7 × 5 = 35	0 × 2 = 0	4 × 10 = 40	4 × 4 = 16
1 × 9 = 9	5 × 10 = 50	2 × 3 = 6	5 × 3 = 15
9 × 3 = 27	6 × 2 = 12	5 × 6 = 30	7 × 1 = 7
10 × 2 = 20	1 × 1 = 1	3 × 6 = 18	5 × 8 = 40
4 × 0 = 0	3 × 8 = 24	6 × 4 = 24	2 × 5 = 10
2 × 7 = 14	1 × 5 = 5	7 × 3 = 21	9 × 4 = 36
3 × 10 = 30	8 × 0 = 0	5 × 5 = 25	8 × 2 = 16

PAGE 15

8 × 2 = 16	0 × 6 = 0	3 × 3 = 9	4 × 6 = 24
2 × 4 = 8	7 × 3 = 21	5 × 4 = 20	1 × 9 = 9
2 × 5 = 10	6 × 5 = 30	4 × 10 = 40	3 × 4 = 12
1 × 2 = 2	7 × 4 = 28	4 × 4 = 16	9 × 2 = 18
8 × 3 = 24	2 × 2 = 4	2 × 3 = 6	7 × 1 = 7
2 × 10 = 20	9 × 0 = 0	6 × 3 = 18	3 × 9 = 27
1 × 4 = 4	8 × 4 = 32	6 × 6 = 36	3 × 5 = 15
9 × 4 = 36	10 × 3 = 30	0 × 1 = 0	5 × 7 = 35
2 × 7 = 14	9 × 5 = 45	6 × 2 = 12	5 × 10 = 50

PAGE 16

START ↓

3 × 7	2 × 5	2 × 2	5 × 4	8 × 2	7 × 1
10 × 2	9 × 0	5 × 6	1 × 10	2 × 6	5 × 7
5 × 5	2 × 8	4 × 10	3 × 8	5 × 10	4 × 9
4 × 7	3 × 3	9 × 2	7 × 2	4 × 4	2 × 6
9 × 3	4 × 2	2 × 3	3 × 5	8 × 4	3 × 4

FINISH ↓

PAGE 17

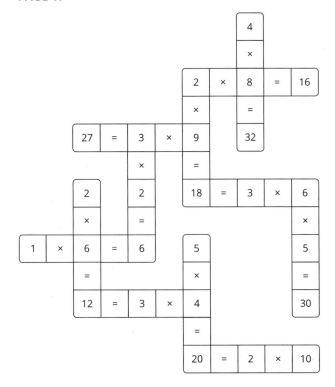

PAGE 18

6 × 5 = 30	6 × 2 = 12	6 × 4 = 24	7 × 6 = 42
4 × 6 = 24	8 × 6 = 48	9 × 6 = 54	1 × 6 = 6
6 × 6 = 36	3 × 6 = 18	6 × 5 = 30	9 × 6 = 54
2 × 6 = 12	5 × 6 = 30	1 × 6 = 6	6 × 4 = 24
10 × 6 = 60	6 × 1 = 6	6 × 3 = 18	6 × 7 = 42
6 × 2 = 12	6 × 8 = 48	6 × 7 = 42	6 × 6 = 36
6 × 9 = 54	3 × 6 = 18	6 × 10 = 60	4 × 6 = 24
6 × 3 = 18	6 × 6 = 36	6 × 9 = 54	6 × 8 = 48
7 × 6 = 42	10 × 6 = 60	8 × 6 = 48	5 × 6 = 30

PAGE 19

7 × 6 = 42	7 × 2 = 14	7 × 10 = 70	7 × 5 = 35
7 × 9 = 63	4 × 7 = 28	7 × 1 = 7	8 × 7 = 56
2 × 7 = 14	7 × 7 = 49	7 × 3 = 21	1 × 7 = 7
5 × 7 = 35	9 × 7 = 63	5 × 7 = 35	7 × 6 = 42
7 × 1 = 7	7 × 3 = 21	4 × 7 = 28	7 × 7 = 49
7 × 4 = 28	7 × 8 = 56	7 × 9 = 63	3 × 7 = 21
7 × 6 = 42	7 × 5 = 35	2 × 7 = 14	10 × 7 = 70
7 × 7 = 49	3 × 7 = 21	8 × 7 = 56	7 × 4 = 28
7 × 8 = 56	9 × 7 = 63	10 × 7 = 70	7 × 6 = 42

PAGE 20

8 × 5 = 40	7 × 8 = 56	8 × 10 = 80	8 × 4 = 32
8 × 2 = 16	1 × 8 = 8	9 × 8 = 72	6 × 8 = 48
8 × 7 = 56	8 × 3 = 24	8 × 4 = 32	8 × 9 = 72
5 × 8 = 40	2 × 8 = 16	8 × 8 = 64	3 × 8 = 24
8 × 1 = 8	8 × 6 = 48	7 × 8 = 56	8 × 10 = 80
4 × 8 = 32	3 × 8 = 24	8 × 5 = 40	8 × 8 = 64
10 × 8 = 80	8 × 6 = 48	8 × 2 = 16	5 × 8 = 40
9 × 8 = 72	8 × 1 = 8	8 × 8 = 64	8 × 7 = 56
8 × 3 = 24	8 × 9 = 72	6 × 8 = 48	4 × 8 = 32

PAGE 21

9 × 3 = 27	5 × 9 = 45	8 × 9 = 72	9 × 2 = 18
6 × 9 = 54	1 × 9 = 9	10 × 9 = 90	8 × 9 = 72
9 × 4 = 36	9 × 3 = 27	9 × 7 = 63	9 × 5 = 45
10 × 9 = 90	9 × 6 = 54	4 × 9 = 36	9 × 9 = 81
9 × 1 = 9	9 × 7 = 63	9 × 9 = 81	2 × 9 = 18
4 × 9 = 36	9 × 8 = 72	6 × 9 = 54	7 × 9 = 63
9 × 3 = 27	9 × 10 = 90	2 × 9 = 18	5 × 9 = 45
9 × 9 = 81	9 × 1 = 9	9 × 4 = 36	9 × 6 = 54
9 × 5 = 45	7 × 9 = 63	3 × 9 = 27	9 × 8 = 72

PAGE 22

10 × 6 = 60	9 × 10 = 90	5 × 10 = 50	10 × 2 = 20
1 × 10 = 10	5 × 10 = 50	10 × 7 = 70	4 × 10 = 40
10 × 10 = 100	10 × 8 = 80	1 × 10 = 10	3 × 10 = 30
10 × 4 = 40	2 × 10 = 20	7 × 10 = 70	8 × 10 = 80
6 × 10 = 60	10 × 7 = 70	10 × 9 = 90	10 × 1 = 10
10 × 3 = 30	10 × 9 = 90	7 × 10 = 70	4 × 10 = 40
10 × 8 = 80	10 × 5 = 50	3 × 10 = 30	6 × 10 = 60
9 × 10 = 90	10 × 2 = 20	10 × 10 = 100	10 × 5 = 50
10 × 4 = 40	10 × 10 = 100	10 × 6 = 60	8 × 10 = 80

PAGE 23

6 × 4 = 24	8 × 2 = 16	5 × 9 = 45	7 × 10 = 70
0 × 8 = 0	3 × 7 = 21	6 × 7 = 42	9 × 2 = 18
8 × 5 = 40	10 × 4 = 40	1 × 9 = 9	2 × 7 = 14
6 × 8 = 48	7 × 7 = 49	7 × 1 = 7	4 × 9 = 36
7 × 9 = 63	9 × 3 = 27	8 × 9 = 72	10 × 2 = 20
8 × 1 = 8	6 × 3 = 18	8 × 10 = 80	6 × 2 = 12
10 × 10 = 100	6 × 9 = 54	6 × 5 = 30	9 × 10 = 90
7 × 5 = 35	8 × 4 = 32	6 × 10 = 60	3 × 8 = 24
7 × 4 = 28	5 × 10 = 50	7 × 8 = 56	9 × 9 = 81

PAGE 24

8 × 8 = 64	9 × 6 = 54	7 × 5 = 35	6 × 6 = 36
6 × 2 = 12	4 × 7 = 28	1 × 9 = 9	2 × 8 = 16
8 × 4 = 32	10 × 5 = 50	9 × 3 = 27	7 × 7 = 49
10 × 9 = 90	0 × 6 = 0	9 × 5 = 45	3 × 6 = 18
7 × 6 = 42	10 × 10 = 100	6 × 8 = 48	9 × 4 = 36
8 × 9 = 72	6 × 4 = 24	9 × 9 = 81	2 × 7 = 14
9 × 2 = 18	7 × 9 = 63	8 × 7 = 56	8 × 0 = 0
7 × 1 = 7	8 × 10 = 80	7 × 3 = 21	6 × 10 = 60
10 × 7 = 70	5 × 8 = 40	5 × 6 = 30	3 × 8 = 24

PAGE 25

10 × 5 = 50	6 × 6 = 36	7 × 3 = 21	9 × 2 = 18
8 × 7 = 56	0 × 7 = 0	8 × 3 = 24	2 × 6 = 12
6 × 3 = 18	2 × 8 = 16	9 × 4 = 36	5 × 9 = 45
9 × 9 = 81	8 × 9 = 72	1 × 6 = 6	2 × 7 = 14
4 × 6 = 24	8 × 5 = 40	4 × 7 = 28	6 × 5 = 30
7 × 9 = 63	10 × 6 = 60	9 × 3 = 27	10 × 8 = 80
8 × 8 = 64	7 × 5 = 35	6 × 7 = 42	9 × 0 = 0
10 × 1 = 10	10 × 10 = 100	4 × 8 = 32	7 × 7 = 49
9 × 10 = 90	6 × 9 = 54	10 × 7 = 70	8 × 6 = 48

Answer key

PAGE 26

5 × 10 = 50	6 × 2 = 12	10 × 7 = 70	2 × 9 = 18
9 × 6 = 54	8 × 8 = 64	8 × 4 = 32	1 × 7 = 7
8 × 10 = 80	4 × 7 = 28	7 × 7 = 49	6 × 1 = 6
2 × 7 = 14	6 × 0 = 0	3 × 6 = 18	5 × 8 = 40
4 × 9 = 36	7 × 9 = 63	6 × 6 = 36	7 × 6 = 42
9 × 1 = 9	9 × 3 = 27	7 × 3 = 21	3 × 8 = 24
10 × 10 = 100	6 × 4 = 24	8 × 7 = 56	10 × 9 = 90
9 × 9 = 81	8 × 2 = 16	9 × 5 = 45	5 × 6 = 30
6 × 8 = 48	7 × 5 = 35	9 × 8 = 72	0 × 10 = 0

PAGE 27

9 × 10 = 90	6 × 7 = 42	9 × 5 = 45	7 × 2 = 14
2 × 6 = 12	9 × 9 = 81	0 × 8 = 0	4 × 8 = 32
7 × 7 = 49	10 × 6 = 60	2 × 9 = 18	6 × 6 = 36
9 × 8 = 72	3 × 7 = 21	6 × 3 = 18	9 × 7 = 63
4 × 6 = 24	10 × 5 = 50	2 × 8 = 16	1 × 10 = 10
7 × 4 = 28	9 × 3 = 27	6 × 9 = 54	5 × 7 = 35
8 × 3 = 24	7 × 0 = 0	8 × 8 = 64	10 × 10 = 100
9 × 1 = 9	8 × 5 = 40	4 × 9 = 36	6 × 5 = 30
7 × 8 = 56	10 × 2 = 20	8 × 6 = 48	4 × 10 = 40

PAGE 28

6 × 8 = 48	2 × 7 = 14	10 × 3 = 30	5 × 9 = 45
8 × 10 = 80	9 × 3 = 27	6 × 2 = 12	3 × 8 = 24
5 × 6 = 30	8 × 7 = 56	9 × 8 = 72	0 × 9 = 0
8 × 2 = 16	6 × 1 = 6	2 × 9 = 18	10 × 7 = 70
7 × 6 = 42	4 × 7 = 28	7 × 9 = 63	6 × 4 = 24
10 × 9 = 90	8 × 8 = 64	9 × 6 = 54	7 × 3 = 21
6 × 10 = 60	3 × 6 = 18	7 × 7 = 49	5 × 8 = 40
10 × 0 = 0	8 × 4 = 32	4 × 9 = 36	6 × 6 = 36
7 × 5 = 35	9 × 9 = 81	1 × 8 = 8	5 × 10 = 50

PAGE 29

8 × 5 = 40	9 × 7 = 63	6 × 3 = 18	7 × 2 = 14
6 × 7 = 42	0 × 6 = 0	5 × 9 = 45	8 × 8 = 64
10 × 8 = 80	8 × 3 = 24	10 × 6 = 60	6 × 5 = 30
10 × 10 = 100	3 × 9 = 27	7 × 8 = 56	9 × 2 = 18
3 × 7 = 21	7 × 10 = 70	1 × 6 = 6	2 × 8 = 16
8 × 9 = 72	7 × 4 = 28	4 × 10 = 40	9 × 0 = 0
4 × 8 = 32	6 × 2 = 12	9 × 4 = 36	8 × 6 = 48
7 × 1 = 7	9 × 9 = 81	5 × 7 = 35	9 × 10 = 90
6 × 6 = 36	10 × 2 = 20	6 × 9 = 54	7 × 7 = 49

PAGE 30

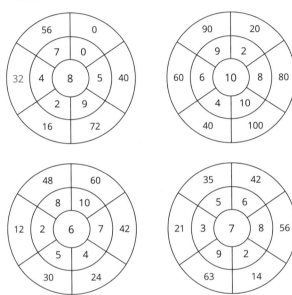

PAGE 31

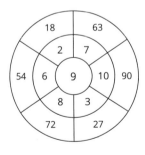

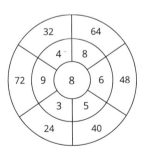

PAGE 32

3 × 4 = 12	7 × 2 = 14	5 × 8 = 40	2 × 5 = 10
6 × 6 = 36	0 × 6 = 0	2 × 3 = 6	5 × 4 = 20
1 × 8 = 8	6 × 3 = 18	5 × 5 = 25	4 × 7 = 28
9 × 10 = 90	2 × 6 = 12	4 × 9 = 36	5 × 3 = 15
4 × 4 = 16	6 × 5 = 30	2 × 4 = 8	4 × 6 = 24
8 × 2 = 16	3 × 3 = 9	2 × 9 = 18	8 × 3 = 24
7 × 5 = 35	10 × 4 = 40	8 × 8 = 64	9 × 5 = 45
8 × 4 = 32	9 × 7 = 63	6 × 8 = 48	7 × 6 = 42
6 × 9 = 54	7 × 3 = 21	7 × 7 = 49	9 × 8 = 72

PAGE 33

5 × 3 = 15	7 × 6 = 42	2 × 5 = 10	2 × 0 = 0
6 × 6 = 36	8 × 5 = 40	3 × 3 = 9	4 × 6 = 24
9 × 6 = 54	4 × 8 = 32	8 × 6 = 48	5 × 9 = 45
4 × 4 = 16	7 × 5 = 35	9 × 9 = 81	9 × 7 = 63
6 × 3 = 18	2 × 8 = 16	4 × 10 = 40	3 × 9 = 27
5 × 1 = 5	7 × 8 = 56	5 × 6 = 30	1 × 4 = 4
10 × 5 = 50	8 × 3 = 24	2 × 9 = 18	9 × 4 = 36
3 × 7 = 21	6 × 2 = 12	7 × 4 = 28	10 × 8 = 80
2 × 10 = 20	0 × 7 = 0	6 × 10 = 60	4 × 5 = 20

PAGE 34

4 × 2 = 8	5 × 5 = 25	3 × 4 = 12	7 × 7 = 49
2 × 7 = 14	2 × 3 = 6	10 × 9 = 90	0 × 2 = 0
6 × 5 = 30	6 × 7 = 42	4 × 7 = 28	8 × 8 = 64
3 × 5 = 15	1 × 9 = 9	5 × 4 = 20	3 × 8 = 24
7 × 9 = 63	10 × 3 = 30	6 × 6 = 36	8 × 4 = 32
5 × 10 = 50	2 × 6 = 12	6 × 4 = 24	3 × 6 = 18
9 × 6 = 54	4 × 9 = 36	5 × 7 = 35	10 × 10 = 100
8 × 5 = 40	8 × 1 = 8	7 × 10 = 70	4 × 0 = 0
7 × 3 = 21	10 × 6 = 60	8 × 6 = 48	8 × 9 = 72

PAGE 35

8 × 8 = 64	6 × 5 = 30	7 × 3 = 21	9 × 10 = 90
7 × 9 = 63	10 × 2 = 20	6 × 7 = 42	2 × 2 = 4
3 × 2 = 6	0 × 5 = 0	9 × 2 = 18	8 × 6 = 48
8 × 4 = 32	9 × 8 = 72	4 × 5 = 20	6 × 6 = 36
5 × 10 = 50	6 × 3 = 18	3 × 1 = 3	5 × 7 = 35
4 × 6 = 24	5 × 2 = 10	10 × 4 = 40	9 × 6 = 54
9 × 0 = 0	5 × 9 = 45	3 × 5 = 15	1 × 8 = 8
10 × 7 = 70	2 × 4 = 8	9 × 3 = 27	4 × 4 = 16
3 × 3 = 9	7 × 8 = 56	3 × 10 = 30	7 × 2 = 14

PAGE 36

3 × 8 = 24	2 × 2 = 4	5 × 6 = 30	7 × 4 = 28
9 × 9 = 81	6 × 4 = 24	0 × 3 = 0	8 × 2 = 16
8 × 7 = 56	5 × 10 = 50	2 × 6 = 12	6 × 8 = 48
2 × 4 = 8	8 × 9 = 72	7 × 6 = 42	9 × 5 = 45
6 × 9 = 54	3 × 10 = 30	3 × 7 = 21	3 × 4 = 12
1 × 10 = 10	7 × 5 = 35	9 × 4 = 36	2 × 9 = 18
3 × 9 = 27	6 × 0 = 0	3 × 6 = 18	10 × 7 = 70
5 × 5 = 25	8 × 4 = 32	2 × 7 = 14	5 × 3 = 15
9 × 7 = 63	7 × 1 = 7	10 × 4 = 40	5 × 4 = 20

PAGE 37

5 × 9 = 45	8 × 3 = 24	3 × 7 = 21	6 × 6 = 36
7 × 1 = 7	6 × 9 = 54	6 × 2 = 12	5 × 0 = 0
4 × 3 = 12	7 × 9 = 63	8 × 5 = 40	10 × 3 = 30
8 × 8 = 64	0 × 6 = 0	5 × 4 = 20	5 × 2 = 10
6 × 8 = 48	4 × 9 = 36	10 × 6 = 60	4 × 6 = 24
3 × 3 = 9	10 × 5 = 50	9 × 8 = 72	10 × 9 = 90
2 × 10 = 20	6 × 5 = 30	3 × 2 = 6	9 × 2 = 18
1 × 3 = 3	4 × 2 = 8	3 × 9 = 27	10 × 1 = 10
7 × 10 = 70	7 × 5 = 35	2 × 8 = 16	4 × 7 = 28

PAGE 38

PAGE 39

  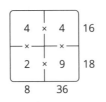

3 × 7 = 21	2 × 5 = 10	4 × 4 = 16
9 × 4 = 36	7 × 4 = 28	2 × 9 = 18
27 28	14 20	8 36

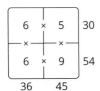 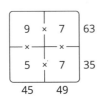

6 × 5 = 30	9 × 7 = 63	6 × 8 = 48
6 × 9 = 54	5 × 7 = 35	3 × 3 = 9
36 45	45 49	18 24

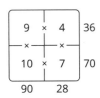 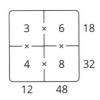

9 × 4 = 36	3 × 6 = 18	8 × 9 = 72
10 × 7 = 70	4 × 8 = 32	7 × 6 = 42
90 28	12 48	56 54

PAGE 40

4 × 9 = 36	6 × 6 = 36	7 × 5 = 35	2 × 7 = 14
6 × 8 = 48	1 × 6 = 6	9 × 8 = 72	3 × 3 = 9
9 × 9 = 81	3 × 4 = 12	7 × 7 = 49	2 × 4 = 8
2 × 3 = 6	5 × 8 = 40	7 × 6 = 42	9 × 3 = 27
5 × 10 = 50	9 × 5 = 45	9 × 0 = 0	8 × 7 = 56
5 × 5 = 25	8 × 4 = 32	10 × 6 = 60	5 × 6 = 30
9 × 6 = 54	3 × 10 = 30	4 × 5 = 20	10 × 4 = 40
0 × 7 = 0	8 × 8 = 64	7 × 9 = 63	8 × 1 = 8
2 × 5 = 10	6 × 2 = 12	8 × 10 = 80	10 × 2 = 20

PAGE 41

8 × 9 = 72	2 × 7 = 14	10 × 10 = 100	8 × 4 = 32
2 × 6 = 12	5 × 9 = 45	3 × 10 = 30	6 × 5 = 30
7 × 7 = 49	4 × 4 = 16	8 × 2 = 16	5 × 0 = 0
9 × 10 = 90	1 × 2 = 2	3 × 6 = 18	6 × 7 = 42
3 × 5 = 15	7 × 3 = 21	2 × 3 = 6	8 × 8 = 64
0 × 3 = 0	4 × 6 = 24	5 × 5 = 25	10 × 7 = 70
7 × 5 = 35	9 × 9 = 81	7 × 9 = 63	5 × 4 = 20
6 × 6 = 36	3 × 4 = 12	4 × 7 = 28	10 × 4 = 40
3 × 8 = 24	5 × 10 = 50	2 × 4 = 8	9 × 6 = 54

PAGE 42

10 × 2 = 20	8 × 9 = 72	5 × 5 = 25	7 × 8 = 56
9 × 3 = 27	7 × 6 = 42	9 × 0 = 0	6 × 3 = 18
2 × 2 = 4	6 × 4 = 24	8 × 6 = 48	9 × 9 = 81
7 × 4 = 28	1 × 6 = 6	4 × 9 = 36	6 × 5 = 30
6 × 6 = 36	9 × 7 = 63	4 × 5 = 20	10 × 3 = 30
4 × 3 = 12	5 × 8 = 40	7 × 10 = 70	5 × 3 = 15
0 × 7 = 0	6 × 2 = 12	5 × 7 = 35	8 × 1 = 8
2 × 5 = 10	4 × 4 = 16	6 × 9 = 54	3 × 7 = 21
8 × 8 = 64	2 × 4 = 8	8 × 10 = 80	9 × 5 = 45

PAGE 43

9 × 8 = 72	8 × 7 = 56	4 × 6 = 24	8 × 8 = 64
0 × 3 = 0	3 × 4 = 12	5 × 9 = 45	5 × 10 = 50
4 × 7 = 28	10 × 10 = 100	2 × 8 = 16	4 × 1 = 4
3 × 9 = 27	8 × 3 = 24	6 × 6 = 36	6 × 8 = 48
5 × 6 = 30	1 × 2 = 2	3 × 5 = 15	7 × 9 = 63
10 × 9 = 90	3 × 6 = 18	7 × 5 = 35	3 × 2 = 6
6 × 7 = 42	8 × 5 = 40	5 × 0 = 0	7 × 3 = 21
9 × 4 = 36	7 × 7 = 49	4 × 8 = 32	6 × 2 = 12
4 × 2 = 8	9 × 6 = 54	2 × 5 = 10	5 × 5 = 25

PAGE 44

9 × 9 = 81	6 × 5 = 30	7 × 6 = 42	4 × 3 = 12
3 × 8 = 24	6 × 9 = 54	1 × 7 = 7	5 × 10 = 50
4 × 5 = 20	4 × 4 = 16	8 × 6 = 48	5 × 7 = 35
0 × 6 = 0	10 × 3 = 30	9 × 7 = 63	4 × 6 = 24
8 × 9 = 72	6 × 6 = 36	2 × 5 = 10	8 × 8 = 64
2 × 2 = 4	7 × 4 = 28	5 × 8 = 40	9 × 3 = 27
10 × 8 = 80	9 × 1 = 9	2 × 4 = 8	3 × 7 = 21
7 × 7 = 49	6 × 3 = 18	9 × 5 = 45	8 × 0 = 0
4 × 9 = 36	8 × 4 = 32	3 × 3 = 9	2 × 10 = 20

PAGE 45

2 × 2 = 4	8 × 7 = 56	9 × 4 = 36	4 × 10 = 40
5 × 9 = 45	2 × 8 = 16	1 × 3 = 3	7 × 7 = 49
10 × 10 = 100	5 × 6 = 30	6 × 8 = 48	9 × 6 = 54
0 × 2 = 0	4 × 4 = 16	3 × 5 = 15	6 × 7 = 42
3 × 6 = 18	7 × 5 = 35	9 × 8 = 72	6 × 4 = 24
8 × 1 = 8	10 × 9 = 90	3 × 4 = 12	5 × 4 = 20
7 × 9 = 63	3 × 2 = 6	6 × 6 = 36	4 × 0 = 0
4 × 8 = 32	5 × 1 = 5	9 × 2 = 18	8 × 5 = 40
5 × 5 = 25	4 × 7 = 28	8 × 3 = 24	9 × 9 = 81

PAGE 46

				START ↓	
3 × 6	5 × 3	2 × 3	4 × 8	9 × 6	4 × 7
6 × 5	6 × 2	5 × 8	8 × 7	1 × 9	9 × 3
5 × 9	7 × 6	8 × 9	5 × 3	2 × 2	1 × 7
4 × 6	5 × 2	7 × 3	3 × 4	6 × 6	4 × 4
2 × 8	4 × 5	4 × 9	8 × 8	7 × 9	5 × 5

FINISH ↓

PAGE 47

= 3   = 5   = 6   = 9   = 5   = 2

= 6   = 8   = 4   = 10   = 2   = 7

= 7   = 8   = 4   = 9   = 6   = 3

PAGE 48

8 × 8 = 64	3 × 5 = 15	9 × 8 = 72	6 × 0 = 0
6 × 8 = 48	6 × 5 = 30	10 × 10 = 100	2 × 4 = 8
5 × 7 = 35	3 × 3 = 9	7 × 6 = 42	9 × 4 = 36
6 × 6 = 36	5 × 4 = 20	10 × 7 = 70	8 × 5 = 40
3 × 2 = 6	7 × 9 = 63	0 × 5 = 0	5 × 5 = 25
5 × 9 = 45	9 × 9 = 81	8 × 7 = 56	4 × 6 = 24
7 × 1 = 7	4 × 8 = 32	7 × 4 = 28	9 × 6 = 54
4 × 3 = 12	3 × 9 = 27	1 × 8 = 8	7 × 7 = 49
4 × 4 = 16	2 × 10 = 20	6 × 3 = 18	3 × 7 = 21

PAGE 49

8 × 9 = 72	0 × 8 = 0	4 × 7 = 28	3 × 3 = 9
10 × 3 = 30	8 × 6 = 48	9 × 9 = 81	5 × 3 = 15
2 × 2 = 4	6 × 7 = 42	7 × 8 = 56	8 × 10 = 80
7 × 5 = 35	2 × 3 = 6	9 × 7 = 63	2 × 7 = 14
9 × 1 = 9	3 × 4 = 12	4 × 4 = 16	7 × 0 = 0
3 × 6 = 18	7 × 7 = 49	5 × 6 = 30	8 × 4 = 32
5 × 5 = 25	6 × 2 = 12	6 × 9 = 54	4 × 5 = 20
2 × 8 = 16	9 × 5 = 45	8 × 8 = 64	4 × 9 = 36
5 × 8 = 40	1 × 10 = 10	6 × 4 = 24	6 × 6 = 36

PAGE 50

9 × 9 = 81	7 × 4 = 28	9 × 2 = 18	5 × 1 = 5
4 × 6 = 24	3 × 3 = 9	9 × 8 = 72	2 × 8 = 16
8 × 5 = 40	5 × 9 = 45	6 × 5 = 30	8 × 8 = 64
10 × 10 = 100	5 × 7 = 35	0 × 4 = 0	7 × 6 = 42
5 × 4 = 20	7 × 7 = 49	4 × 3 = 12	6 × 8 = 48
3 × 0 = 0	3 × 2 = 6	4 × 4 = 16	3 × 7 = 21
7 × 9 = 63	8 × 7 = 56	5 × 10 = 50	3 × 5 = 15
5 × 5 = 25	10 × 4 = 40	1 × 6 = 6	9 × 6 = 54
4 × 8 = 32	6 × 6 = 36	9 × 4 = 36	6 × 3 = 18

PAGE 51

9 × 10 = 90	5 × 2 = 10	4 × 7 = 28	8 × 9 = 72
5 × 8 = 40	7 × 0 = 0	2 × 2 = 4	3 × 6 = 18
4 × 4 = 16	9 × 5 = 45	7 × 8 = 56	3 × 8 = 24
7 × 5 = 35	6 × 9 = 54	8 × 8 = 64	5 × 6 = 30
9 × 9 = 81	3 × 4 = 12	9 × 3 = 27	0 × 6 = 0
6 × 4 = 24	3 × 3 = 9	10 × 6 = 60	6 × 7 = 42
1 × 8 = 8	9 × 7 = 63	8 × 4 = 32	6 × 6 = 36
5 × 5 = 25	8 × 6 = 48	3 × 10 = 30	9 × 1 = 9
7 × 2 = 14	4 × 9 = 36	7 × 7 = 49	4 × 5 = 20

PAGE 52

9 × 6 = 54	4 × 8 = 32	6 × 5 = 30	4 × 4 = 16
3 × 7 = 21	10 × 10 = 100	8 × 5 = 40	5 × 10 = 50
5 × 5 = 25	5 × 4 = 20	0 × 3 = 0	9 × 8 = 72
2 × 4 = 8	6 × 6 = 36	7 × 4 = 28	6 × 2 = 12
4 × 0 = 0	3 × 2 = 6	8 × 2 = 16	9 × 9 = 81
7 × 9 = 63	6 × 8 = 48	3 × 3 = 9	5 × 7 = 35
8 × 8 = 64	4 × 3 = 12	5 × 9 = 45	1 × 5 = 5
7 × 6 = 42	6 × 1 = 6	4 × 6 = 24	10 × 6 = 60
9 × 4 = 36	8 × 7 = 56	5 × 3 = 15	3 × 9 = 27

PAGE 53

11 × 3 = 33	11 × 5 = 55	6 × 11 = 66	8 × 11 = 88
11 × 1 = 11	10 × 11 = 110	11 × 9 = 99	11 × 3 = 33
4 × 11 = 44	11 × 7 = 77	11 × 4 = 44	11 × 9 = 99
11 × 11 = 121	2 × 11 = 22	11 × 6 = 66	1 × 11 = 11
6 × 11 = 66	11 × 10 = 110	11 × 11 = 121	7 × 11 = 77
11 × 8 = 88	11 × 4 = 44	3 × 11 = 33	11 × 2 = 22
11 × 0 = 0	9 × 11 = 99	11 × 7 = 77	5 × 11 = 55
11 × 11 = 121	11 × 10 = 110	11 × 8 = 88	2 × 11 = 22
9 × 11 = 99	1 × 11 = 11	11 × 5 = 55	6 × 11 = 66

PAGE 54

1 × 12 = 12	12 × 4 = 48	12 × 2 = 24	6 × 12 = 72
7 × 12 = 84	8 × 12 = 96	1 × 12 = 12	10 × 12 = 120
2 × 12 = 24	12 × 7 = 84	3 × 12 = 36	0 × 12 = 0
6 × 12 = 72	12 × 1 = 12	12 × 9 = 108	12 × 8 = 96
4 × 12 = 48	11 × 12 = 132	12 × 3 = 36	12 × 5 = 60
12 × 9 = 108	12 × 12 = 144	5 × 12 = 60	12 × 3 = 36
12 × 12 = 144	12 × 8 = 96	4 × 12 = 48	0 × 12 = 0
9 × 12 = 108	12 × 10 = 120	12 × 5 = 60	12 × 6 = 72
3 × 12 = 36	12 × 0 = 0	12 × 11 = 132	2 × 12 = 24

PAGE 55

12 × 6 = 72	6 × 11 = 66	9 × 12 = 108	12 × 0 = 0
7 × 11 = 77	12 × 11 = 132	0 × 12 = 0	9 × 11 = 99
11 × 5 = 55	11 × 2 = 22	12 × 7 = 84	0 × 11 = 0
1 × 12 = 12	11 × 11 = 121	2 × 11 = 22	5 × 12 = 60
12 × 12 = 144	11 × 7 = 77	11 × 12 = 132	4 × 11 = 44
11 × 1 = 11	12 × 3 = 36	12 × 8 = 96	12 × 10 = 120
11 × 11 = 121	12 × 2 = 24	6 × 12 = 72	8 × 12 = 96
12 × 4 = 48	11 × 4 = 44	3 × 12 = 36	11 × 9 = 99
8 × 11 = 88	7 × 12 = 84	10 × 11 = 110	12 × 12 = 144

PAGE 56

12 × 8 = 96	0 × 12 = 0	12 × 12 = 144	7 × 11 = 77
1 × 11 = 11	12 × 6 = 72	11 × 10 = 110	12 × 9 = 108
11 × 7 = 77	12 × 7 = 84	11 × 11 = 121	11 × 4 = 44
12 × 1 = 12	11 × 0 = 0	12 × 5 = 60	12 × 12 = 144
11 × 8 = 88	6 × 12 = 72	12 × 0 = 0	11 × 6 = 66
10 × 12 = 120	12 × 4 = 48	11 × 1 = 11	2 × 12 = 24
3 × 11 = 33	11 × 12 = 132	9 × 11 = 99	11 × 5 = 55
12 × 2 = 24	11 × 9 = 99	4 × 12 = 48	11 × 2 = 22
12 × 3 = 36	5 × 11 = 55	12 × 11 = 132	8 × 12 = 96